AI SIMPLIFIED

ARTIFICIAL INTELLIGENCE: UNDERSTANDING IT AND MAKING YOUR LIFE EASIER

ALBERT HSU

TABLE OF CONTENTS

INTRODUCTION

When I was a kid, I played with used punch cards that my dad brought home from work. He used them to write stock market analysis programs on a mainframe computer used at his job. I didn't realize then that those cards were part of the early days of modern computing, but today, they're pretty much gone. In 1983, I bought my first computer and had only used a computer at school for computer science courses. It was a new Apple IIe with 64 KB of RAM using 5.25-inch floppy disks and came with a Hayes 300 baud modem, which all seemed futuristic. Now, all those things have vanished too.

Personal computers used to be huge and heavy with green, glowing screens. Back then, artificial intelligence was only in science fiction stories. Today, most people use AI, and it's becoming more involved in our lives. I've watched AI grow and change over the last four decades, from simple programs to complex systems. I don't think many people know software like **ChatGPT** and **Midjourney** is the result of sixty years of research and billions of dollars spent on AI in all its forms.

My goal is to make AI less scary, something that everyone can understand and use. AI is everywhere now, but it still seems confusing to many people. To help you understand it, I'm going to explain what AI is and why it is how it is, at least in my view.

AI is changing our lives, not in obvious ways that some people might notice right away, but in many small changes that everyone keeps making, almost like they don't notice. If you want to know what life will be like in two years, just look at what people are doing with AI right now. The momentum continues to build.

WHAT IS AI?

Artificial intelligence, or AI for short, is when we make machines that act like they're smart. Of course, "smart" means they can do things like play chess well, understand and talk back to us, or pick the next movie we'll enjoy watching. AI learns from data and adjusts to new information. It does jobs that we usually think only humans can do, like writing reports, diagnosing problems in cars, or finding our best friends' photos in all the pictures someone has.

AI is already deeply woven into the fabric of our everyday lives. It's there when we ask our phones for the weather, and it understands our voice; it's there when we get the best-personalized product suggestions while shopping online; and it's certainly there when we listen to music or watch movies, and we don't have to pick what to listen to or watch because AI curated our playlists or movie suggestions. In fact, AI is there when we do any of these things because AI makes these tasks easier and more suited to us.

To most people, it doesn't feel like a robot is serving us, but rather a human. AI has lots of benefits, but it also has some worries. For example, people are afraid of losing jobs and privacy, and many questions arise about what will happen if AI becomes too smart. But if we make sure to put important things like transparency, privacy, and ethics first, we can see that the benefits probably outweigh the risks, at least right now. For one thing, AI creates jobs. Even if some jobs disappear from AI that is automating tasks we do now, new jobs are already on the rise.

The potential of AI is almost limitless. AI can help improve health-care by making treatments more suited to each person. It can make education better by personalizing learning experiences. It can even help save the environment by making climate models more accurate and making green products and energy sources more effective. AI is here to help us do things better, not to replace us.

This book begins with basic ideas about AI and gradually moves toward more complex ones. We will build on each chapter, and by the end, you will understand AI better and see how it can be used in good ways and what real-world problems it can solve. We will also talk about ethical problems, both real and imagined, that have already surfaced and are likely to surface.

I hope you will be open-minded. Even if you know a little about AI or nothing at all, I want to provide you with knowledge and give you confidence—knowledge about what AI is and what it can do now and confidence to go look deeper into it yourself. So, let's go on this journey together. We'll see how AI can help improve our lives. Thank you for joining me!

1

UNDERSTANDING THE BASICS OF AI

Many years ago, I managed investment portfolios for several large multi-billion-dollar groups. During this time, I met with a hedge fund manager who showed an AI system capable of analyzing a wide range of data, including economic indicators, interest rates, political risks, commodity information, corporate data, and asset pricing. This system could find investment opportunities by processing vast amounts of information at unprecedented speeds, achieving analysis that would be impossible for a human. I recognized both the immediate benefits and the potential of this technology.

AI had not been used this way in finance so comprehensively. But I quickly saw that there was no way a human could compete with the technology in speed or the sheer amount of data being processed. What I witnessed was the direction for the future: more technology-assisted investing along with more investment opportunities.

WHAT IS ARTIFICIAL INTELLIGENCE?

Artificial Intelligence (AI) is when machines mimic human intelligence. This simple definition includes many technologies and ways that AI can be used. At its core, AI aims to create systems that do tasks that usually need human smartness. These tasks include learning from experience, recognizing patterns, and making decisions. Unlike traditional software that follows fixed rules, AI software changes and improves as it processes more data. AI is the part of computer science that tries to mimic human skills. For example, it can help diagnose diseases, analyze medical images, and even create personalized treatment plans in healthcare. In finance, it detects fraud and decides where to invest. In entertainment, we use AI in video games. It gives us interesting stories, and it makes animated characters act and look almost lifelike. If you think AI is only about robots or if you confuse it with machine learning, you aren't alone. Machine learning is just one part of AI. It's the part that involves training computers to learn from data and improve over time.

KEY TERMS AND CONCEPTS EXPLAINED

To grasp why AI works the way it does, you need to know some key terms. **Machine learning** is one of the most talked about, which means using algorithms that let computers learn from data. For example, the spam filter in your email gets better at recognizing unwanted emails by looking at lots of data and finding patterns. This ability to learn and improve is why machine learning is a big part of AI. But there's another important idea: **neural networks.** Think of them like a system that imitates how the human brain works. In neural networks, layers of interconnected nodes, like neurons, process the data. They are especially good at tasks that require recognizing complex patterns, such as identifying images and understanding speech. For example, if you upload a photo to social media, a neural network might be used to recognize faces or tag objects in the picture. A type of AI that uses many layers of a neural network for even more complex tasks, like natural language understanding or self-driving cars, is called **deep learning**.

THE EVOLUTION OF AI: A BRIEF HISTORY

In the 1950s, British mathematician **Alan Turing** started the whole idea of AI by suggesting a "thinking machine." He came up with the **Turing**

Test to see if a machine could act like a human. The term "**Artificial Intelligence**" didn't even exist until the 1960s. Then, at the **Dartmouth Conference**, AI officially became its own field. Researchers in those early years poured their hopes into a program, trying to figure out how to code human knowledge into computers. Writing down human knowledge in a way that a computer could use and then making it "think" like a human turned out to be much harder than they thought.

The project got a boost in the 1980s when researchers started using neural networks and machine learning. These methods allowed systems to learn from data. Now, big breakthroughs in AI are mostly about finding patterns in vast amounts of data.

2

AI IN EVERYDAY LIFE

Imagine getting a medical diagnosis that ends up saving your life, thanks to a computer program that detected something unusual about you. This is happening now, changing healthcare and other aspects of our lives. Cancer can be diagnosed much sooner using artificial intelligence that catches the early signs before symptoms appear. AI has the potential to save many lives who suffer from life-threatening diseases. We hear that artificial intelligence is revolutionizing medicine now, but AI has been around for a long time.

AI IN HEALTHCARE: REVOLUTIONIZING DIAGNOSIS AND TREATMENT

Artificial intelligence is completely changing the practice of medicine. The impact of AI on today's healthcare is impossible to measure because it's happening in real time. It is already affecting diagnoses and treatments. The changes are impressively fast and, in many ways, seem more accurate than what skilled and experienced doctors can do. But the real revolution, the quiet kind that changes everything, starts with medical imaging. AI promises to change how we detect diseases over many years. Its promise, however, is present and immediate. Many amazing things are happening with diagnostic imaging and computers.

AI is helping doctors give better treatment plans for each person. Using computers to read tons of health data isn't just figuring out a disease. It's also finding the best ways to treat someone as a unique person. The most important data is genetic info from the patient and their family. This tells us which treatments will work and which won't. Soon, AI might help find the best diabetes treatment. It will look at the many different ways each person's body can develop and respond to this disease. Diagnosing diabetes isn't the biggest task of AI in healthcare. It's just one example.

AI is having a big impact on many areas, but one area that benefits from AI is drug discovery. This area provides a great deal of new knowledge that helps the whole field. Developing a new drug usually takes ten to fifteen years and costs about $2.6 billion. AI can reduce both the time and cost. AI can run simulations to predict how a drug will behave in the human body. It can predict if a drug compound will be toxic or not. And AI can do all this way faster than human researchers.

AI is also helping doctors and hospitals guess what will happen in the future and stop problems before they happen. This is called **predictive analytics**, and it works great with AI. Predictive analytics works by looking at patterns in huge amounts of past data. It tries to find the cause of events that have often happened before. For example, AI can study a patient's health history and other important information to predict if they will need to return to the hospital after being discharged.

Here's a true story: Researchers at MIT made an AI system that predicted breast cancer up to five years before diagnosis. The system was trained only on the normal ones and learned to recognize the very subtle signs of cancer. Even when the AI made mistakes, it was only wrong in the same way as the experts who reviewed the results.

AI in healthcare is about more than just technology. It's about improving the care patients receive and the decisions doctors make. AI helps us detect diseases faster and better. It's making healthcare more precise and effective. It's discovering new drugs and repurposing old ones, all while making treatments more personalized and accessibly tailored to each patient.

AI IN ENTERTAINMENT: PERSONALIZING YOUR EXPERIENCE

Imagine if you opened **Netflix** and found a list of shows and movies that

were created just for you. It might seem like magic, but it's AI working behind the scenes. Every time you start or stop watching a series or watch something all the way to the end, the recommendation algorithm pays attention to your tastes and preferences. It uses all the data about what people are watching to guess which shows or movies you might like next. Netflix isn't the only platform that uses AI algorithms to recommend content. **YouTube** and **Spotify** do the same thing.

AI's influence on entertainment goes beyond the things you watch or listen to. It has already begun to change the gaming world. In today's video games, AI helps create dynamic characters. These characters respond to the player in real time. Actually, they interact with the player better than most humans can. In the best games, they are smart and adaptable. They learn your tricks and counter them. You've probably played a game that used AI like this.

AI is increasingly being used to make art, music, and writing. For example, AI-created music is super popular right now. But even if you listen to music made by machines, is it real music? I often ask myself what defines art? The question of what art is might seem boring, but it's important for understanding how art has been thought about over the years.

There are also interactive art displays powered by AI. You might see these at art shows or festivals. Picture a piece of art that changes if you move or interact with it. These AI art pieces use sensors. Most of the time, they sense movement. But what if a piece of art could tell if you were smiling? Or if it could change in front of you because it understood your facial expression? These kinds of interactions might make AI art more exciting. But is "exciting" what we want from art?

AI isn't just about efficiency in entertainment; it's about personalization and enhancing creativity. It's what decides what you watch on Netflix and how you interact with video games or art displays. It's making your experiences more tailored, interactive, and engaging. Think about the computer science challenges that many talented people are solving right now.

AI IN SMART HOMES: MAKING LIFE CONVENIENT

Imagine a home where everything is perfectly set up for you even before you wake up. The temperature is just right, the lights come on gradually so they don't hurt your eyes, and the coffee is brewing at just the right moment. These aren't just dreams anymore. With smart home technology and AI, our houses can easily do these things. Smart devices learn our habits over time. They figure out when we're home or away. They know how to adjust things, not just for comfort but also for efficiency, which often means saving energy (and money).

AI is making a big difference in home security. Smart security cameras can tell the difference between friendly faces and possible intruders. This means they can know who to let in and who to keep out. These cameras work with AI, and they watch over homes day and night. They give their owners peace of mind that almost nothing will get past them.

Voice-activated assistants, like **Alexa, Google Assistant**, and **Siri,** play a big role in smart homes. These assistants do a lot more than just answer questions; they help control other smart devices in our homes. For example, you might ask a voice-activated assistant to do different things while you're cooking dinner. You could tell it to change the temperature, dim the lights, and play your favorite song. Then, without lifting a finger, you let the assistant handle it all.

It's not just about making our lives comfortable and convenient. Managing our energy use is a big part of living an "intelligent" lifestyle. Many AI systems help us with this by tracking how much energy we use and giving us helpful advice on how to use less. They do this in real time, often guiding us through decisions that have both good and bad outcomes (things we can control vs. things we can't, like the weather). And many of these systems let us feel good about ourselves for making the right choices. Feeling good about ourselves is an important part of using AI to improve our lives.

If you're thinking about making your home smarter, install a smart thermostat. You'll hardly notice it working, but it will keep your home cozy all year round. If you're like most people, you have some things that need the power always on, like Wi-Fi routers and security cameras. Using smart plugs to control these devices lets you cut your home's power use in half. Once you start exploring the universe of smart plugs and switches, you'll see how smart lighting is at the core of a fully connected home.

3

HANDS-ON WITH AI

When I started looking into AI, I was mostly excited but a little unsure. I had all these cool new tools to play with but no instructions on how to use them. So, I tried some of the easier platforms to see what happened. I quickly learned that AI isn't as hard to get into as I thought. Even though some people act like you need a computer science PhD to understand it, you can start working with AI and understand how things fit together pretty well without one. In this chapter, I want to show you some beginner-friendly AI tools and projects that are fun to explore.

GETTING STARTED WITH AI: BEGINNER-FRIENDLY TOOLS

If you've ever wanted to make an AI project but thought coding would be too hard, some tools are great for beginners. Let's look at two of these tools: **Google Teachable Machine** and **Microsoft Lobe**.

Teachable Machine by Google is one of the easiest tools for making AI models. If you want to learn about machine learning in a hands-on way, you should definitely check it out. It's an online tool that lets you create models using images, sounds, or even poses—without coding. If you want to teach a computer to identify different types of fruits, like apples, bananas, and oranges, you can do it super quickly with Teachable Machine. Basically, just take some photos of each fruit, upload them to the platform, and hit "train." In a few minutes, you'll have a model that can tell which fruit is which.

Even **Microsoft's Lobe**, another easy-to-use tool, shows how image classification works. Lobe's job is to make this as easy as possible. I mean easy. You drag and drop. That is literally how I used it (my images weren't literally my own, but were close enough). In case you need more convincing to try it out, Lobe doesn't use coding.

After you drag and drop, Lobe successfully analyzes your images, trains a model, and shows you results when you use it again with different pictures. With each step, you see what's happening without getting lost in complicated stuff. It's a good show, and you don't have to worry about the coding at the end. You can just watch and learn.

Here's a clear and easy guide to help you understand how to use Teachable Machine:

Gathering and Sharing Information: Imagine you want to teach an AI to tell different pets apart. First, you need a bunch of good pictures. You can take photos with your phone or find and download them from the internet. Make sure you only use photos that you took yourself or that are okay to use (like public domain images).

You can easily train a computer model by doing these simple steps. First, upload a bunch of pictures to Teachable Machine. It's important to have enough images so the model learns well. You shouldn't expect the model to recognize a cat unless you've uploaded at least a few images of cats. And these images should be different enough that they show several kinds of cats so the model understands what a cat looks like.

You can test the model's ability to recognize new images. This means you take some pictures and upload them to see if the model recognizes them. If you get good results, and I hope you do, you can export the model and use it in your own projects. This might be for a website, a mobile app, or possibly other places like a desktop app.

Another area AI is exploring is creating simple chatbots. Using platforms like **Chatfuel** and **BotStar**, you can build chatbots without coding. Instead, they use an easy drag-and-drop interface. This lets you decide what the bot says in response to users. For example, you could make a bot to answer common questions on your site, or you could use it to help people with basic customer service tasks.

It's a good idea to begin with a simple AI tool that's easy to understand. From there, you can pick AI projects that match what you have set up on your computer and how much you know about coding. If you feel confident, you can tackle more complex challenges.

DIY AI PROJECTS: SIMPLE EXPERIMENTS TO TRY AT HOME

Making AI stuff at home is a great way to learn and have fun. Here are a few easy DIY AI projects to check out:

1. **Create a simple system that recognizes images.**

   You could easily make a simple system that tells different kinds of pets apart, like dogs, cats, and birds. First, get pictures of the pets you want to identify. Then, use **Google Colab** to write codes that tell the system how to recognize the pets.
   You can upload your own pictures to Google Colab and then use a ready-to-go neural network model (like MobileNet) to train your system to tell the difference between animals. This project shows you how AI "learns" by finding patterns in pictures.

2. **Make a tool that analyzes people's feelings.**

   Another interesting thing you can make is a sentiment analysis tool, which is a system that looks at text and figures out if it's positive, negative, or neutral. You could work on this project with a friend or a group. Start by getting some text data, like movie reviews or social media posts. Then, use Python and libraries like **NLTK** (Natural Language Toolkit) or **TextBlob** to train your model to recognize sentiment.
   For example, we could use it to look at Twitter posts about our favorite sports team and see if fans are mostly happy or kind of mad after the recent games. This is a perfect way to start understanding how AI figures out what we mean when we say something.

3. **Make a sound-activated assistant.**

   Developing your own AI personal assistant lets you pick exactly what features you want. It will be tailored to your specific needs. You can use the **SpeechRecognition** library in **Python** to write a program that listens to your voice. It will understand simple commands and do tasks for you, like telling you what the weather is like today. It will also set reminders. Start by having it tell you the time. When you get better at it, add more functions. If you want to, you can even use basic machine learning.

4. Manage tasks and schedules.

One of the best AI task organizers is **Todoist**. Todoist learns from your own habits and helps organize your tasks better. It even suggests when you should work on some tasks to keep you moving toward your goals. Another helpful AI tool is Clockwise. This tool doesn't help with tasks, at least not directly. But it does help you use your time better so you can reach your goals faster. The way Clockwise does this is pretty cool. It basically moves your meetings around in time and space.

5. Manage your email.

Dealing with emails seems like a never-ending job. They're everywhere and seem to multiply when you try to get rid of them. What if we had a tool that used AI to divide the emails we got into important ones and unimportant ones? Use **SaneBox** (or a tool like it) to split your emails into two groups, and your inbox would look way cleaner. SaneBox helps you with your overloaded inbox and works with any email service. It sorts your incoming emails and puts them into different folders. The tool uses artificial intelligence to figure out which emails are the important ones you should read right away and which ones can wait. SaneBox also lets you set up "reminder" emails. These are emails that you get again later to help you remember to follow up on them.

6. Pay attention, and don't let anything distract you.

If you can't concentrate, AI can help with that, too. Programs like **Freedom** and **StayFocusd** use AI to block websites that distract you while you work. There's also **Focus@Will**, which uses AI to pick music that scientific research says will help you focus. It's an excellent way to use AI.

7. Manage a project.

If you're in charge of projects or teams, you can make your work easier by using AI tools like **Trello** and **Asana**. These tools work with AI to analyze schedules, assign tasks, and find possible spots where the project might get stuck. By using these tools, you bring smart, future-thinking helpers into your project management. AI can find project delays even before the people involved notice them.
Here's a checklist you can use to get started with using AI tools to be more productive:

- Download and install **Todoist** to manage your tasks.
- You should use **Clockwise** to arrange your schedule.
- To reduce distractions, use **Focus@Will** or **Freedom**.
- In order to make project management easier, integrate AI tools into **Trello** or **Asana**.

These tools can help you manage your time better, keep up with tasks, and reduce interruptions. They can make your work hours more efficient and less stressful.

These DIY projects help you practice with AI, making it less scary. It's one thing to hear about AI developments in the news and another to see what they can do when you use them yourself. If you want to understand how AI works, the best way is to get your hands dirty. Experiment with these DIY mini-projects, and maybe you'll think of some cool upgrades to make them better.

4

ETHICAL CONSIDERATIONS AND AI

Think about getting an interview for a job you want and then never hearing back. Later, you find out that an AI recruitment tool didn't select you because you didn't meet its personal "fit" criteria, even though you were probably good enough for the job. This isn't a crazy story. It's happening a lot in recruitment today. It's the latest way that big companies, especially in tech, have found to help them hire people quickly without any human involvement. If something goes wrong, at least they won't have to deal with a pesky human getting in the way.

UNDERSTANDING AI BIAS: CAUSES AND CONSEQUENCES

There are lots of ways AI can be biased, but they almost always start with the data we train the AI on. If the training data has historical biases, then the AI will learn and repeat those same biases. For example, an AI might make smarter choices about who to hire in the future if it looks at past hiring decisions. But if the

past hiring was biased, then the AI might keep those biases or even increase them when it makes future hiring decisions.

AI bias can also happen when humans collect data. When people are involved, they can unintentionally let their own biases show in the data. For example, if we gather images to train a system, we might only pick images of people who are very light-skinned. Or if we label images of people with very dark skin, we might not do it equally. This happens because the people doing the work may not realize their own biases or because they're not being supervised well.

The design of AI algorithms further complicates the issue. Since people make these algorithms, they can show their creators' biases if fairness isn't prioritized. For example, an AI recruitment tool might favor resumes with certain keywords. These words happen to be more common in male candidates, which leads to unintentional gender bias. This clearly shows that AI developers must make fairness and bias awareness core values and work hard to achieve them.

Biased AI systems can cause big problems. AI tools that check job applicants can discriminate against people based on irrelevant things like their appearance. They can also be used in bad ways if we aren't careful. Some people worry that the government might use them to invade our privacy. For example, people might be stopped just because they look different from the usual. Imaging programs then match them to AI-generated suspicious facial features. Also, critics have pointed out that ChatGPT and similar systems are prone to hallucinating, making up nonexistent facts and events, and offending users on a daily basis.

Addressing AI bias requires effective ways to accomplish that goal. One promising method is using fairness metrics. These are methods that check if an AI's predictions are fair across different groups. These groups can be defined in many ways, but the most important are the basic ones: gender, race, and background, which are often called "protected categories." However, just using fairness metrics (which, by the way, can be very confusing) isn't enough.

Regular checks are super important. By watching an AI system all the time, we can find and fix the biases that pop up even in the best systems, making sure the system is running properly. This way, we earn the trust of the people using it.

Case Study: AI Bias in Criminal Justice and Finance

The **Correctional Offender Management Profiling for Alternative Sanctions (COMPAS)** is used in our criminal justice system. It is used to determine the probability of a criminal reoffending. A complex algorithm, it was later determined that it had unfair racial bias and rated African American defendants as more likely to offend when compared to white defendants with similar pasts and records. The harsher treatment of these Black defendants, who were given more "high-risk" labels, demonstrates that biases in AI software have a serious, real impact on people's lives.

For example, some AI systems that score credit have been biased against women. These systems gave men better scores than women, even when their finances were the same. Because of this, some women were unfairly turned down for loans or got worse loan terms. When bias happens like this, it's not just a numbers problem. It's a human problem. It clearly shows why we need to solve bias in AI systems.

PRIVACY CONCERNS IN THE AGE OF AI

Imagine a world where everything you say and do is recorded and analyzed. It's not too far from the world we live in today. AI-powered devices and services collect a ton of information about us, from our browsing habits to where we are and what we like. While this data helps make user experiences better (like improving how a smart assistant works), it also brings up privacy concerns. The more data is gathered, the more appealing it is to hackers and the more useful it becomes for surveillance.

Artificial intelligence surveillance is moving out of our personal devices and into public areas. Cities all over the world are using AI-driven CCTV cameras to boost security. These systems promise better, faster, and more helpful monitoring. But what about privacy? It's meant to keep us safe, but does it make us feel like we're always being watched? For people who see surveillance and think *Big Brother*, these AI systems might be the biggest "Big Brother" we've ever seen.

To deal with these worries, laws about privacy have been created. One of the most complete privacy laws is the **European Union's General Data Protection Regulation (GDPR)**. It gives people the most power over their own data. Basically, the GDPR says that you aren't allowed to collect someone's personal data without their permission. Once you have permission, you have to be clear about what you're going to do with the data and how you're going to use it. Similar to the GDPR, the **California Consumer Protection Act (CCPA)** gives California residents power over their personal data. According to the CCPA, California residents have the right to know what personal data is being collected about them, why it's being collected, and who has access to it.

In the age of AI, how can we protect privacy and protect data? How can we safeguard our most private moments? AI systems are making huge advancements and are being used in countless ways to analyze personal and sensitive data. This is exactly what privacy advocates have warned us about for years. The **National Institute of Standards and Technology (NIST)** has issued guidelines on how to handle data safely. One recommendation is to use "privacy-preserving techniques." These methods blend data protection with useful analysis of the information.

Encryption is very important to keep data safe while it's being stored and sent. If we want to make sure that data doing its job in our computers isn't seen by anyone it shouldn't be seen by, we need to encrypt it. This is the way to do it.

Real-World Example: Privacy Breaches in Health Apps

A recent example is a popular health app that had a data breach. This app, used by millions of people to track their fitness, seriously failed in protecting data. The app's users had their sensitive health data exposed, including not only sleep patterns but also how much they moved and overall activity levels. What is even more troubling is that the app, like many others in this area, had terms of service that gave it permission to share user data with third parties. It also made promises about keeping data confidential that it evidently failed to uphold.

ETHICAL GUIDELINES FOR RESPONSIBLE AI DEVELOPMENT

We need fairness, transparency, and accountability in AI. These main ideas help us use AI responsibly. We are committed to making AI that doesn't discriminate, and if it does, it's because of the data we provide, not the system itself. Also, if we can understand why AI makes a decision, we can likely make it better and improve our own decision-making.

Being open means AI systems are set up in a way that people get what's going on, especially how decisions are made, and actions are taken. When talking about loan applications, if a computer program denies someone a loan, an open AI would be able to give a clear answer to the question, "Why was I refused?"

Ensuring that AI treats all groups equally is what many people think "fairness" means. Developers can make sure their AI systems are fair by using diverse datasets and checking their systems for biases.

AI systems need to be responsible for what they do, and there should be no doubt about who is accountable. If an AI makes a mistake or causes harm, there must be a way to understand what happened, fix it, and hold someone responsible. This is especially true in important areas where humans should always supervise, like medical diagnoses or the criminal justice system. These are places where the consequences of AI mistakes are very serious.

Collaboration is crucial. We need people from different fields—like ethicists, sociologists, and legal experts—to make sure the AI systems we build are ethical. Sometimes, we also need to include people from communities that the AI affects. For example, we involved people from the communities that the facial recognition system, which was being developed at the time, would affect. Collaborating with all these people improves the next steps.

Many guides and resources to develop ethical AI are already available. For example, the **Ethical Advised Design** created by the **Institute of Electrical and Electronics Engineers (IEEE)** is an important document. It provides principles for building fair, clear, and responsible AI systems. **AI4People's Ethical Framework** is also very important. It was created by **AI4People**, a group supported by the European Union. It is clear that the purpose of AI should be to help society.

5

AI IN CREATIVE ARTS

Picture yourself in an art gallery. You walk up to a painting. It's beautiful and seems to glow with life. You can see the colors mixing together on the canvas. There are clear details in the painting that make your eyes move around it. It makes you think about what's happening and maybe even try to understand it in a new way. This painting could also be a drawing or even a digital artwork. But I want you to imagine it as a painting because that's what I'm most comfortable with when I think about art.

AI IN ART: FROM CREATION TO CURATION

AI-generated art is one of the most exciting ways that technology meets creativity. What's making this amazing new development possible? It's **Generative Adversarial Networks** or **GANs**. They are made to create original artwork. GANs use two neural networks: one that makes images and another that judges them and gives them a score. The network that makes images is called the generator, and it tries to make art that looks human-made. The judging network is called the discriminator. It's like an art critic (except it's an artificial one) that compares the fake art to the real thing. The discriminator sends feedback to the generator, telling it how to improve. This cycle keeps going until it makes art that's almost the same as what humans would create.

Artificial intelligence (AI) is playing a part in more than just making new art; it's also getting used in art restoration. AI is helping experts find the best way to fix historical paintings.

Restoring old art is hard and needs extreme precision, both in the tools we use and the skills of those doing it. This is because the best restorers try to make their repairs as invisible as possible, so viewers can't tell where the original ends and the restoration begins.

AI can help with this challenge because, well, it's AI. AI can "see" patterns and understand what's happening in an image. An AI program developed at MIT, for example, gained attention for its ability to analyze frescoes, a type of wall painting.

One of the places where AI is used is in choosing art. Usually, a curator's job is to arrange and show artworks using their own knowledge. But now, AI can help by checking art styles, historical contexts, and even what visitors prefer. For example, an AI system might look at thousands of artworks and notice connections and similarities that people wouldn't find. People might not think, for instance, that a Van Gogh painting is similar to a Monet, but AI can. People might not see that two paintings, one from Africa and one from Europe, are both about the same theme. But AI can because it knows what both paintings are about.

Interactive AI art setups are getting more popular. They create immersive experiences by responding to how viewers move and what they feel. In 2019, I visited an AI-driven Van Gogh exhibit in New York City. The AI art installation there used motion sensors to keep track of everyone in the room. Using these sensors, it changed which Van Gogh "pieces" were shown on the walls. It had "intelligent" ways of deciding which person to show next and which pieces fit best with the exhibit's theme.

Case Study: AI-Powered Art Installation at Digital Art Festival

An interactive AI art show set up at a digital arts festival was almost too perfect. At least, that's what the audience seemed to think. People who moved more often found different results than those who were still. This happens partly because of the motion sensors that the AI artists relied on. These sensors not only recorded movement but also tracked people, measuring how much interaction they produced to get credit with the AI.

MUSIC AND AI: COMPOSING THE FUTURE

Think about a future where hit songs aren't written by people but by AI. This isn't some distant future; it's happening now. AI is already making millions of songs. AI programs can figure out the structure, melody, and harmony of a pop song. They analyze thousands of existing hits and create new ones. Some of these songs are so good that they might fool us into thinking they were made by famous songwriters. AI can also write music for symphonies and operas like Beethoven. Overall, AI's music is better than you'd expect, but can AI-generated songs mimic those written by a human or evoke feelings like a human song can? AI's music could be pleasant to listen to. It might sound good because it follows rules that make melodies catchy and harmonies pleasant.

Artificial intelligence is changing music production, too. For example, **LANDR** is an AI-powered platform for mixing and mastering tracks. It analyzes songs to make sound quality better. This saves music producers time. Now, AI can help with creative tasks, but mostly, it helps with sound setup jobs. AI might take over more of the setup work soon, but producers are excited about using intelligent systems in creative ways.

AI isn't just helping people make music; it's also changing how we find and enjoy it. Music platforms like **Spotify** (which is the biggest one) have been using algorithms for a long time to recommend music to people based on what similar users have liked in the past. But now, those algorithms are getting even better because Spotify is using AI to upgrade them.

An especially cool thing about AI in music is getting to work with humans and AI together. AI gives musicians great ideas, like catchy melodies and fresh chord progressions. But it also helps musicians see new possibilities in the music they already make.

AI's help means that being a musician now is different from what it used to be. Musicians can not only compose songs but also think about what their music could become. They do all this with the help of computers, both smart and not-so-smart.

Case Study: AI-Human Collaboration in Music

A good example of humans and AI working together is the album ***I AM AI*** by **Taryn Southern**. Taryn teamed up with an AI called **Amper Music** to make the songs. The AI came up with the basic music, and Taryn added her voice and lyrics. Together, they created an interesting mix of human and machine music, with over ten tracks that tell a story. Working with AI made Taryn Southern a more creative person. She shows us that AI can help create art, not just tools that replace painters, musicians, or writers.

WRITING WITH AI: ENHANCING CREATIVITY

In writing, tools powered by AI are important. They help us with grammar and style and even create stuff for us. Real writing assistants use AI to understand how humans write and what they value. When we use them, we hope they'll make our writing better or at least help us avoid some grammar mistakes. But what kind of help do AI assistants give? That totally depends on the kind of AI they are and the kind of writing we're doing.

When writing, people work closely with their computers. Our computers help us come up with ideas, organize our thoughts, and find the right words. Computers have always been tools for writing. AI can be a tool, too. But when AI itself starts writing, it becomes a different kind of tool.

AI is not just helping writers; it is creating full articles and other written work itself. Some news companies are using AI to write simple news stories. These companies save money because AI does not need to be paid like a person. They make more money because they can publish more since AI works faster than humans. AI costs less, so they can publish more and sell more ads. AI is already a big part of the problem for people who write news.

AI tools can be helpful for coming up with ideas and brainstorming. If you have to write a boring paper about some ancient historical event, AI won't help you much. I'm sure some smart professor figured out how to make that assignment interesting to their students and how to grade it fairly. But you still have to do the work. There are big ethical and moral issues when we start using AI to write.

6

AI IN EDUCATION

Think about a classroom where every student's unique needs are not just noticed but fully met. A place where lessons adapted in real time, or almost so, seemed not only like a distant dream but also beyond what most teachers would think possible. This is taking shape at the hands of AI in education. An AI-powered platform can help teachers better understand their students than ever before. This has deep and profound implications for education as it provides customized education for each student.

PERSONALIZED LEARNING WITH AI

Personalized learning is changing education for students who learn best when things are adapted to their individual needs. In the past, education considered people in groups, like by age. And teaching was pretty much the same for everyone. But now, we know that not everyone learns in the same way or at the same speed. Personalized learning tries to make it so everyone can learn in a way and at a speed that works best for them.

To add some technical terms, personalized learning uses computers and artificial intelligence to make the best "learning path" for each student. A "learning path" is the order and kind of things a student learns. This also includes how they learn it. Personalized learning tries to figure out the best "learning path" for each student.

Many adaptive learning platforms, like **Knewton** and **DreamBox**, are at the forefront of personalized education. They actively adjust to each student as the student interacts with the platform. Knewton, for example, uses its AI to analyze whatever data it can find about the student. Then, it recommends a personalized order of topics for the student to learn and relearn. Knewton tries to find out what the student doesn't know and gives them virtual flashcards to remember it. DreamBox takes a different approach. It works mostly with students in grades K-8 (kindergarten through eighth grade) to help them learn math. Unlike Knewton, which is a platform that supports various subjects, DreamBox is completely focused on math instruction.

Artificial intelligence is important for personalized learning, and formative assessments are another key part of that. Formative assessments are given during the learning process to check how much students are understanding. AI can help here. For example, AI can make quizzes and practice tests just for you. These assessments are timed to give you immediate feedback. Formative assessments are sometimes called "low-stakes" because they don't usually (or shouldn't) add up to a final grade. So, the low-stakes environment lets you focus on your improvement, learning to correct and avoid mistakes in future assessments.

When making a curriculum, AI helps teachers create personalized courses that fit each student. AI looks at key educational standards and lots of student data. Then, it picks the best content for each student's unique learning goals. And when we say "content," we don't just mean the main stuff in the curriculum. We mean any kind of teaching material. For example, an AI tool might suggest a harder book that checks the same ideas as the one in the main reading for a student who is ahead in writing skills. Or it might find an easier book that has the same main ideas for a student who needs more help in writing.

Case Study: Improved Student Outcomes Using Adaptive Learning Technology

A pilot program in a diverse urban school district shows how effective adaptive learning technology can be. For their K-8 math curriculum, the district used DreamBox. Over the school year, students using DreamBox had a 30 percent increase in math proficiency compared to their classmates in traditional classrooms. Teachers in the case study shared that the real-time adjustments and personalized feedback were helpful because they kept students engaged and focused on the math tasks. This is one way we can see how artificial intelligence could enhance the educational experience for students and teachers.

By using AI in personalized learning, we are pushing for a fairer and better education system. AI algorithms look at how students perform and their learning styles, then change lesson plans and study materials to fit each student. Adaptive learning platforms like Knewton and DreamBox adjust what students work on in real time, responding to how they perform as they do it. Other AI tools give immediate feedback and help with certain topics when a student needs it the most, right after they first try it. In making curricula, AI helps teachers create paths through lessons, using course materials that fit each student's needs so they can reach their goals.

AI TUTORS: ENHANCING STUDENT ENGAGEMENT

Academic support for students is getting a new twist. AI is stepping in where human tutors used to be, giving students real-time help with homework and study questions. When the math problem you're staring at seems impossible, and there's no one around to help, that's when the AI tutor should show up. At least, that's what we thought would happen.

Real human math tutors, and even the **Tutors of the Future** (like **Carnegie Learning's MATHia**, which is also AI-driven), focus a lot on understanding the problem before finding a solution. The idea is to let the student figure it out with just the right guidance.

AI tutors can improve student engagement and learning. They do this by offering instant and personal support. The support doesn't have to be perfect; it just needs to be reasonable. What's more important is the immediate feedback that keeps students from getting bored. AI tutors explain things in different ways. Some students need a good visual to understand. Others do better when things are clearly explained in writing. AI tutors can be all these things: visual, verbal, and everything else, depending on what the student needs at that moment.

Natural Language Processing, or **NLP**, is the main technology that helps AI tutoring systems work. For one main reason, it's very important. NLP is the reason AI tutors can have simple, kind-of-like human conversations with students. When a student asks a question, the AI tutor understands what is asked. Then, it works through the context, both the question and what came before it, to give an answer that's not only correct but also relevant in a natural way that makes the student feel understood. You can see this in language learning apps like **Duolingo**.

AI tutors make working together easier for students and help with group study sessions. AI can set up and lead study groups, keep the conversations on track and make sure everyone stays involved. It's like being with a supersmart friend who makes sure no one in the group gets too lazy while studying together. A good AI study buddy will push you to explain things clearly, keep talking until you both understand each other well and make you feel kind of silly if you don't try your best to solve a problem before asking for help. Tools like **Google's Socratic** show us how smart helpers can boost student teamwork.

To get the most out of AI tutors, keep these suggestions in mind:

1. For regular practice and to strengthen what you're learning, use AI tutors consistently.
2. To get clear answers, you should ask specific questions. Instead of saying, "Explain Newman's fly," ask it like this: "How does Newman's fly show natural selection?" The second question needs someone to think more deeply and give a better answer.
3. Mix AI tutoring with regular studying to cover everything you need to be ready for tests like the SAT and ACT.
4. Get involved in study groups that AI sets up to make working together in study groups better.
5. Give comments on how the AI tutor is doing so we can make the system better.

If you want to make the most of AI tutoring systems and get a better learning experience, add these practices to your study routine.

AI tutoring systems are a strong solution for getting students more involved and improving how they learn. AI tutors give real-time, personalized help to students so they always have someone to turn to. Interacting with speech-based, local natural language processing AIs feels more human. These interactions promote engagement and increase the chances of collaborative learning. When you dive into AI tutors, you realize how different, engaging, and efficient these learning tools are.

THE FUTURE OF AI IN EDUCATION

Picture a classroom where, instead of just reading about history, students are living it through virtual reality. This kind of immersive experience, which makes you feel like you're part of something real, is becoming possible in education thanks to new AI technologies like virtual and augmented reality. You might have heard of some of these AI tools, like ChatGPT, that can make human-like text and have conversations. Today, "AI" usually means algorithms that can predict the next word in a sentence. But we also have other kinds of AI that work with visual information, creating images from text descriptions or even generating whole virtual worlds and the stories in them. And if you think this might be a little creepy, you're not alone; many people do.

Another example of AI in education is predictive analytics, which is used to help at-risk students. By looking at patterns in student data like attendance, grades, and how much they engage with school, AI can tell which students might fall behind. Then, teachers can give help before any problems get worse. Many schools have seen good results with this. Some have helped almost all their at-risk students move up a grade. Others have made sure that most students who start college finish their first year.

Lifelong learning and professional development are being changed a lot by AI. In today's fast-moving world, we need super current education. Our skills and knowledge have to be up to date and almost continuously improved. AI offers us a powerful new tool to help us learn throughout our lives and grow professionally.

Now, you might ask, how exactly does AI help us learn better? Well, one way is through personalization. AI allows us, or our AI partners, to create a totally fit learning experience. Actually, we're just at the start of this journey. The things we have today are super impressive already, but they still don't reach the full potential of AI in personalization.

Fairness in education is another area where AI shows huge promise. Underserved communities often have bad luck when it comes to quality education. Their students might have good reasons to wonder why a good school is so far out of reach. They don't have the resources or qualified teachers to help students thrive. What if AI could change that? The first step is to bridge the crazy gap in schooling equity across America. After that, we can look at other countries. AI tools can be the missed opportunity turned into a bridge. They offer students in remote, poor, and underserved places high-quality educational content, and pretty much for free if you think about it.

We face challenges and ethical issues, such as making sure AI is fair and unbiased. Another problem is using AI while keeping students' private information safe. They must develop strong ways to protect sensitive student data. Are we using these systems to help everyone equally, or are we making things worse and leaving some students behind? These are ethical questions we have to think about. Even though AI is used to make decisions, humans are still very much involved. Educators must stay in charge of the ethical reasons that should always be part of choosing AI. This is an important part of using it in education.

7

AI IN BUSINESS

In the past, when we needed help from a company, we had to call them and wait on hold until someone was free to talk to us. But now, when we call, we might get an AI chatbot that can talk to us instead of a person and help us with our problems. Sometimes, these AI-powered chatbots can help you solve the problem seamlessly, but as of now, 100 percent has not been achieved.

AI IN CUSTOMER SERVICE: CHATBOTS AND BEYOND

Today, AI chatbots are the most important part of customer service. They are always available and give instant answers to all sorts of questions. They help with many tasks, from tracking orders to getting product information. The best thing about AI chatbots is that they help people right away, at any time. So, they are service agents who work all the time without any breaks or pay. They are good at performing the service that most humans can't do because they can't work all day.

Advanced features are helping AI customer service bots do more than just handle simple inquiries. Because of this, our interactions with these bots are becoming more personalized and satisfying. **Natural Language Processing**, or **NLP**, is a key technology that lets chatbots understand and respond to complex questions like a human would. NLP understands the subtlety and complexity of human speech or writing. This allows chatbots to pick up on the context of a question. For example, if you ask, "What's the best way to return a damaged item?" the chatbot understands that you're asking for specifics about the return process and the steps involved. Sentiment analysis is another advanced feature that gauges customer emotions during interactions. A chatbot can't see your face or body language, but it can analyze the tone of your message to tell if you're happy, sad, or angry.

Another new thing is predictive customer support. Predictive customer support looks at customer behavior patterns to guess what problems might happen in the future and tries to fix them before they even start. One example is an AI virtual assistant predicting subscription renewals. Your AI assistant knows you're about to renew your $30 annual subscription to a website. Your assistant messages your bank's AI to check for suspicious activity and if there are enough funds to renew. If there aren't any issues, the bank can pay the renewal and inform your AI assistant that the renewal was successful.

Case Study: Real-World Examples of AI in Customer Service

Companies that sell products online have quickly started using AI chatbots to improve their customer support. Now, we see companies using these chatbots for several tasks. Chatbots are good at handling simple questions when many customers contact a company. AI can make chatbots even better, helping them understand and respond like humans do. When they're used well, AI chatbots help customers and improve a company's efficiency. Whether return policies are too complicated, constant shipping updates make you feel like a package stalker, or product info is hard to find, these AI helpers lend us a virtual hand.

In the financial world, companies like **Bank of America** are using AI chatbots to help manage customer accounts. Bank of America's AI assistant, Erica, is available 24/7 to help its customers. Erica helps customers with things like checking their account balances and moving money between different accounts. Sometimes, she even helps people make payments. Instead of just being a clever but simple virtual assistant, Erica tries to be more like a financial advisor to the bank's customers.

AI is changing customer service in big ways. AI chatbots and other smart tools are giving customers instant help that's tailored just for them. They also offer support that's not only reactive but also proactive. This means businesses are finding new ways to serve their customers even before they ask for help. And these AI helpers are getting smarter all the time. So, the possible gains of AI in customer service, both for businesses and their customers, are amazing.

AI IN MARKETING: TARGETING AND PERSONALIZATION

Imagine walking into a store and finding everything there is made just for you. That's the kind of personalization we're getting, thanks to AI in marketing. Today, personal things like seeing a friend's name pop up when you open your phone are normal. With AI, people can have lots of cool stuff, like targeted ads that seem perfectly timed and smart virtual assistants that can chat like a person and understand our natural speech. But these breakthroughs are just the start of what's possible, and some people worry that as AI in marketing gets better, it might become more invasive.

AI is making a big change in personalized marketing campaigns. Now, marketers can use AI to fit almost every part of a message to each specific audience member. These personalized messages seem to reach people at the right moments and on the right channels. For example, AI-powered email marketing tools can look at vast amounts of data to decide which products to recommend to someone. And they do this at a scale and speed that humans just can't match. For example, if someone checked out three pairs of running shoes on a website but didn't buy them, an AI system might figure out that the person is likely to look at running shoes. So, it sends an email with a great deal on one of the pairs they checked out. When you add up all the ways marketers can make personalized messages with AI, it gets impressive.

Artificial intelligence greatly helps with marketing on social media. AI tools help with posting schedules, analyzing how people respond to posts, and optimizing content so it reaches as many people as possible. AI can even help come up with content ideas. Using AI for idea generation can be efficient, whether you're using a tool that generates image ideas, video ideas, or all kinds of written ideas. This is because, for a long time, we've known that coming up with many new ideas is a key part of finding good marketing ideas. Since AI is great at generating lots of content that looks pretty real, you should definitely try using it to help create your marketing campaigns.

AI provides great benefits in the area of marketing automation. Tasks like scoring leads and sending marketing emails are done with amazing precision and speed. Here's how it works: **HubSpot, Marketo**, and other marketing automation platforms manage advertisements and budgets for thousands of companies. They decide which projects to fund. They also figure out how to allocate resources among many different strategies to get the best results. Humans have always done these jobs in the past. Now, smart software can do them. And that's a good thing. AI can help pick the best leads, nurture them, and make them more likely to convert. It can do all these things well.

AI is changing marketing, and businesses are figuring out how to use it because it helps them connect better and faster with customers. AI is mainly good at two marketing tasks: figuring out which people are in an audience, dividing them into subgroups, and personalizing messages for each person. AI can also help scale up brands by giving them better insights from social media and automating repetitive tasks that take too long for humans.

AI IN SUPPLY CHAIN MANAGEMENT

Artificial intelligence is changing supply chain management by making processes better and cutting costs. This isn't just about using powerful AI to analyze data. It's mostly about all the smart algorithms figuring out and dealing with demand. These algorithms are what's making supply chains smarter now. AI is a great tool for intelligent demand forecasting. Predicting how much customers will want is the hardest, most important, and often most underrated part of supply chain management. If you mess up forecast demand, it messes up everything else. AI helps because it analyzes and compares what's happened in the past with what might happen in the future. Then, it creates insights that lead to better decisions.

When it comes to logistics and transportation, AI offers great opportunities for improving efficiency and speeding things up. If you could ask the top people at **UPS, FedEx**, and the **U.S. Postal Service** what they dreamed about when they were young, I bet they never imagined they would one day run the world's biggest delivery services. Each company sends out about 20 million packages every day, and they all deal with problems like traffic jams and bad weather that make deliveries late and cost too much money. But every single day, by using a totally awesome combination of human skills and AI-powered plans, these three companies get more done in less time and with fewer resources than anyone else in the world. They don't actually use the word "AI" much. Those letters don't even show up on the dashboard of any of their route-planning software. And that's smart because the less we think about AI, the more we realize its potential.

Just like other areas of business, managing suppliers can also use artificial intelligence or AI. Many AI tools are already helping with supplier relationship management, and even more are expected to come out soon. Some of these tools analyze historical data to predict how reliable and good a supplier will be in the future. The best tools study relevant data from a variety of sources and use it to find the best supplier for a specific need. After signing contracts, other AI tools help monitor how well the supplier is doing. They do this by looking at performance data that the company and the supplier share. Some tools even check data from outside sources to see how the supplier is doing compared to others.

Another important area where AI is helpful is managing risks. AI models try to predict possible problems by looking at things like market changes, world events, and even natural disasters. These models send out early warnings. But they're not so much about "You might be at risk" and more like "We can see there's a risk, and here's what we think is causing it." So, companies get all these extra insights. They get early warnings. And they can usually handle anything that could hurt them or their supply chains. When companies can keep running, no matter what, world peace is on the rise. And you might say we're on a path to a tornado-free future, which is good for all of us.

8

AI AND THE JOB MARKET

Imagine getting to your office, and instead of doing the same boring tasks every day, someone tells you that your AI-powered assistant is going to handle all the repetitive stuff for you. You can spend your working hours mostly on creative projects and making important plans instead. You're definitely not alone in hoping this will be part of our not-so-distant future.

WILL AI TAKE MY JOB? SEPARATING MYTH FROM REALITY

People often worry that AI will take away lots of jobs, but this fear is usually blown out of proportion. If history teaches us anything, it's that big technology changes create new kinds of work instead of getting rid of jobs altogether. For example, some jobs disappeared during the Industrial Revolution, but many new ones were created. Machines took over simple, boring tasks so workers could use their minds more and do more interesting things. AI in business might be doing the same thing now. It isn't replacing computer programmers and other "knowledge workers." Instead, AI is taking over routine tasks those workers used to do.

Some industries will be impacted a lot, while others will see smaller changes. Manufacturing, logistics, and customer service will probably be the most affected. In manufacturing, AI-powered robots assemble products with precision, reducing mistakes and improving productivity. In logistics, AI optimizes delivery routes and manages inventory, helping companies save time and money. Finally, in customer service, AI chatbots handle common questions so that human staff can solve more complicated problems.

Creative jobs are hard for machines to do. Imagination and emotional understanding are needed in art, writing, and music. Machines can't do these like humans can. They might help us do them better, but they can't replace us. We would be much better off if creative people used AI as a tool instead of letting AI generate art, music, or stories on its own. AI could assist in healthcare. But if your surgery is done by a robot, you will still want post-operative care from a nurse.

AI could change jobs a lot. It can take over boring, repetitive tasks, letting people do more interesting and meaningful work. But law firms are looking into using AI for tasks that are still done by junior lawyers—you know, basic stuff like research and writing first drafts. AI can insert information and write sentences that sound pretty natural. But it can't understand what that information means. For now, at least.

AI is beginning to help people at work in many areas. It was first used in stupid ways, like chatbots that couldn't understand or help with complex problems. But now, it's getting smarter. For example, in jobs that need specialized knowledge, like in law and medicine, we're seeing AI used more intelligently. It's helping with problems that are hard to understand and fix. AI has gotten better at interpreting images, diagnosing diseases, and predicting outcomes.

Interactive Element: Reflect on AI in Your Industry

Think about how AI might affect your industry. Here are some things to consider:

1. What everyday tasks in your job could AI help automate?
2. How could AI give you more time to focus on strategy and creativity?
3. Are any new jobs popping up in your field because of AI?
4. How can you get ready to adapt to the changes that AI will bring?

If you ask yourself these questions, you'll probably start to see how AI might not only shape your career but also make growth opportunities more obvious for you.

We are bringing AI into the workforce not to replace jobs but to change them. Instead of AI doing things people usually do, we want people to do things AI can't do well, like creative, strategic, and people-focused tasks. Also, routine jobs will go away, but the people who do them will get new jobs that will help AI be more effective.

FUTURE-PROOFING YOUR CAREER WITH AI SKILLS

In a job market run by AI, people must learn the skills that companies require to be successful. One of the most important skills for a worker today is data analysis. This is the ability to understand huge amounts of data and make decisions based on what it all means. "No matter what field you work in, from marketing and finance to healthcare, being able to understand and analyze data is already a superpower," said **Leslie Gornstein**, a journalist who writes about AI for **The Motley Fool** and other places. "And what data is going to be more important than the data from your own company?"

An important new field is AI ethics. As AI becomes more common, making sure it is used responsibly, especially in ways that aren't biased and that respect privacy, is important. This problem is too big and too important to just be handled by companies building AI systems. We need trustworthy teams of people to make trustworthy AI, and that means we need to teach and train many people in AI ethics.

To keep your career on track, you can't stop learning. The things you used to learn are becoming less and less important. But you have to set aside time, around five hours a week, to learn new skills and keep up in your field. The good thing is that we have lots of ways to keep learning now. You can take mobile courses from almost anywhere. You can keep your head up at work and still get a good pep talk. Even if you go to something like the **AI Expo**, you can see firsthand how the cool new AI toys people are talking about are being put to work in different industries.

In a world ruled by AI, soft skills won't get lost in the noise. They'll continue being super important for all the jobs they could be needed for. These soft skills won't need to be explained in detail because we already know how important they are. AI projects are likely to need much communication. Communication isn't all about talk; it's also about making sure people listen and understand. In a world where people from different backgrounds work on AI projects, communication will be super important.

You can safeguard your career against future changes and stay competitive in a job market affected by AI if you develop a combination of technical skills and the kind of soft skills that can't be easily replaced by machines.

NEW JOB OPPORTUNITIES CREATED BY AI

AI is not only transforming the jobs we have now, but it's also creating completely new ones. For example, people are starting to work as AI ethicists. These new professionals help make sure AI is used fairly and responsibly, which is super important if we want people to trust AI in the future.

There's a new job called "AI trainer." These people help AI systems learn how to do things, like answering questions in customer service. They show the AI examples of questions and answers. This way, the AI learns not just to repeat answers but to understand the problem and find the right answer. AI trainers make sure the AI is always getting better.

Keeping AI up and running means people have to fix problems and update it. Like lots of tech, AI needs these new jobs if we use it in our daily lives. If we want to live happily with AI "**synthespians**" (like those in the TV series ***Humans***), it's good to know someone is keeping the AI world tidy.

AI is also making new jobs that mix different skills. In healthcare, data scientists team up with doctors to make AI tools that improve diagnoses. In finance, analysts use AI to predict trends, and some even claim that AI has become their best financial advisor. These examples show that AI isn't taking jobs away from people. Instead, it's helping industries grow and develop new ways of doing things.

AI is creating new opportunities in entrepreneurship. Startups in healthcare, finance, and retail are using AI to solve problems in smart, creative, and sometimes unexpected ways. Now, healthcare isn't just about jerks in lab coats looking at data on people like you and me. Actually, an AI startup called **EleutherAI** is working with a creative agency to produce something unusual: a new kind of personalized medicine. Getting your own personalized medicine requires a big change in how we think about healthcare.

Artificial intelligence isn't just changing our work; it's changing the jobs themselves. AI is forming new job areas. It's making old tasks better while also cutting jobs in some places, like in the driverless car industry. But don't start worrying yet because AI promises to create way more jobs than it will destroy. Overall, AI is expected to be amazing for the U.S. economy. By 2030, it could add $7 trillion to $15.7 trillion to the world's wealth.

LET OTHERS KNOW THAT UNDERSTANDING AI IS WITHIN EVERYONE'S REACH

"Artificial intelligence and generative AI may be the most important technology of any lifetime."

— MARK BENIOFF

At the very start of this book, I shared that my main aim was to make AI less intimidating so that you can look well beyond standard services like ChatGPT or Perplexity. I invited you to complete 7 simple tasks using AI in ways you may not have considered before, including creating your sentiment analysis tool and making your own sound-activated system. You have seen how AI can not only save you time but also make you big cost-savings. It's amazing to think that without any coding knowledge whatsoever, anyone can harness the power of AI task organizers, e-mail sorters, and more.

Despite its fast-growing importance, AI education is lagging behind in many companies, both large and small. A vast percentage of the workforce still lacks basic skills in this technology. Statistics show that up to 40% of workers may need reskilling within the next three years due to AI implementation, and even in companies with over 1,000 employees, only 42% have actively deployed AI in their business.

The good news is that you don't have to wait until the powers-that-be at your organization wake up to the need to educate employees on the many functions AI has to offer. You'll be one step ahead... because you'll already know how to harness multiple functions that boost your productivity and enrich your social life and leisure time.

If you feel this book is opening doors to real, practical AI use in your daily life, I'd like to ask you a small favor. Please let others know how you feel.

By leaving a review of this book on Amazon, you'll let other readers know that they don't need a degree in computer science or knowledge of coding to engage AI for greater efficiency and optimal enjoyment.

Thanks for your help. I hope you enjoy the rest of the book, which will show you how AI can be a driving force for positive change in a myriad of sectors, including security, finance, and creativity!

Scan the QR code below

9

AI INNOVATIONS AND FUTURE TRENDS

Imagine driving to work where you don't need to steer, change your route, or even look at the road. You can read your book, catch up on emails, or just relax while your car sails through traffic. This isn't a dream. It's the future that rapid progress in self-driving car technology is bringing closer every day. Cars that drive themselves are being tested on public roads now, and the technology is ready to change how we travel.

AI IN AUTONOMOUS VEHICLES: THE ROAD AHEAD

We've made cool progress in autonomous vehicle technology. **Tesla, Waymo**, and **Uber** are leading the way, and they're all getting closer to fully autonomous vehicles. For example, **Tesla's Autopilot** system has advanced driver assistance features, but it's not the same as the fully autonomous vehicles we're talking about. **Waymo** has been testing self-driving cars on public roads for years. Waymo drivers have taken their cars into many tricky driving situations, like during thunderstorms. Even so, Waymo seems to be ahead in this race among the three companies, which is pretty impressive for an **Alphabet Inc.** subsidiary.

The **Society of Automotive Engineers (SAE)** sets the standards for different levels of automation in self-driving vehicles, from Level 0, which has no automation, to Level 5, where there is full automation. Level 1 has simple assistance for drivers, like cruise control. This is where most cars are today. At Level 2, cars can manage both steering and acceleration but need the driver to watch closely. When we move to Level 3 and then Level 4, cars start handling almost all driving tasks by themselves. But even at Level 4, where the car is more capable, a human driver might need to step in during certain extreme situations. Level 5 has vehicles that can drive themselves in every situation without any help from a human.

Autonomous vehicles need complex and fascinating technology. The main systems in them are **LIDAR (Light Detection and Ranging)** and **radar**. They are very important because they help the car understand its surroundings. They create a 3D map of the environment. This way, the car can "see" in all directions and detect obstacles. The big "decision-maker" is a **machine learning algorithm**. It decides how fast to go, which way to turn, and how to avoid obstacles. The key to this is a technology called **sensor fusion**. Sensor fusion takes data from different sources. These sources include cameras, LIDAR, radar, and GPS. Then, it makes a clear picture of the car's environment. This picture tells the car where it is and what it can do safely and quickly.

Even though self-driving cars are getting better, there are still some problems they need to solve before they can be used everywhere. The first big problem is figuring out how to drive in complicated city traffic. City streets are crowded with people, cyclists, work zones, and many other things. It's a test of brains and brawn—a real obstacle course for anything that calls itself a vehicle. If AI has one big challenge, it's this one. And that's why, in the opinion of many experts, self-driving cars aren't ready to be the main cars people use. Another big obstacle course for AI is the weather.

Society and the economy will be greatly affected by self-driving cars because they will change many things. For example, traffic accidents will probably go down a lot. The number of people killed on the roads each year—more than 30,000 in the U.S. alone —is shocking. What's even weirder is that most of these deaths are caused by human mistakes. But if we think about all the changes the economy will bring, it's clear that self-driving cars will have a big effect on people's incomes. The economy will probably feel more impact when companies like **Uber** start using them, and so will big shipping companies that use trucks for deliveries.

The changes brought by self-driving cars will require new city roads and related infrastructure. Some of these changes could be helpful. They might make things simpler, safer, and more efficient for people, not just for the cars themselves. For example, parking lots could be used for something else. Fewer cars need long-term parking. Meanwhile, using the road space that cars occupy could cut down on traffic, especially where it's bad now. However, the reality of working with these cars, if we plan to control them somehow, could lead to having to build more of some things and redesign others.

Interactive Element: Reflect on Autonomous Vehicles

Let's think about how self-driving cars could affect our everyday lives. Here are some things to consider:

1. What would your daily commute be like if you had a car that drives itself?
2. What benefits and challenges do you think could come from using self-driving cars everywhere?
3. How could self-driving cars affect the number of jobs in your field?

By thinking about these questions, you can start to see how powerful a change to autonomous vehicles could be. This might help you prepare for the shifts that are probably coming.

Independent cars are about to change our travel systems. They promise safer, more efficient, and easier ways for us to get around. But what exactly is an "independent vehicle?" Right now, most of them are just steps toward a future with full AI travel. They use a mix of old and new tech, most of which is still being developed and improved.

THE ROLE OF AI IN CLIMATE CHANGE SOLUTIONS

Predicting severe weather events like hurricanes, floods, and droughts is an enormous challenge. We've used climate models to predict them for a long time. Sometimes, these models are pretty accurate. Other times, they're not. But what if we could make them better? What if we could increase their predicting power? AI has many possible advantages. One of them is using machine learning. These algorithms can see patterns in huge amounts of data—

details that earlier methods overlooked. Maybe this will help improve our weather predictions.

AI is affecting many areas, but one unexpected place is renewable energy. Managing the complex power grid where we send electrical energy is hard. But AI can help make it more efficient. The software lets AI make smart decisions and balance the grid, not just based on how much energy is used in different places but also how much power can be generated. People often forget that the grid is also a storage system. It has to handle energy excess and shortages by either saving power or dumping it into the ground (which sometimes happens with hydroelectric plants). In a smart grid, any generator, like a wind or solar farm, can be seen as a unit that has a certain amount of power it can give now and over the next few hours. AI helps the grid pick where to put the electricity it generates, not by overlooking how much the different units demand and can supply, but by carefully choosing the absolute best places to use the electricity generated.

AI has huge implications in one important area where it can help save ecosystems. For example, monitoring at-risk species has a new tool: AI drones. These drones can cover huge spaces and take amazing, high-definition pictures and videos of animal habitats. Conservationists use this info for two main things: First, they use machine learning to analyze the images. Second, they use an amazing amount of data (pictures, videos, and measurements) to make more and better conservation decisions. If you think that's great, then check this out: AI is also being used to fight illegal logging. AI can recognize activities in satellite images. If it's good enough to find people doing illegal stuff in the forest, then it's definitely doing a great job at saving ecosystems.

Case Study: AI-Driven Climate Initiatives

AI is helping with environmental conservation in many ways. A great example is Google's use of AI to predict and stop deforestation. Google uses its AI system to analyze satellite images and other data. This helps them find places that might soon face deforestation. Then, by working with governments and organizations, they can make plans to save these at-risk forests. This is great because not only do these forests provide homes for many animals and plants, but they also play a vital role in controlling the Earth's climate. When trees are cut down, they release carbon that contributes to global warming. Google isn't the only tech company in this environmental conservation race.

Think about an Earth where climate prediction is so accurate that renewable energy systems not only run smoothly but also work together as a united switchboard, like a state-of-the-art circulatory system ensuring that clean, renewable power flows wherever it's needed.

Picture a world where we're not just guessing about the energy savings and pollution cuts from electric cars. Their environmental impact can be measured so precisely that we know they're helping to cut greenhouse gases.

AI AND SPACE EXPLORATION: EXPANDING HORIZONS

Think about a spacecraft moving through space. It's adjusting its course, making complex maneuvers, and doing all this on its own. This is not just a fun fantasy; it could be our future realization of interstellar evolution. According to **Daniel R. Silberg**, who wrote a paper called "**Artificial Intelligence for Detecting, Tracking, and Mitigating Space Threats**," one big reason our space missions haven't advanced more is that we haven't used AI enough. AI enables many important advancements in trajectory planning and navigation. And when it comes to operating a spacecraft, onboard systems controlling both autonomous and semi-autonomous decision-making tasks are crucial.

AI is playing a central role in pretty much every part of computing —from hardware to software to our own human-time simulations. We need to understand the challenges of working with AI and learn how to solve them if we want to see reliable and impressive results in computing and beyond.

Exploring other planets like Mars has improved because of AI-powered rovers. The **Mars Rover Curiosity** is the perfect example of how AI can change space exploration. It has advanced AI systems that let it do things other rovers can't. Curiosity analyzes surface data, decides on the right spots to collect samples from, and moves through tough terrain without any human help.

Even before these rovers set foot on other planets, machine learning models helped us figure out where they could land safely and find interesting things to study. You can think of an AI model as a kind of intelligent geologist that looks at lots of satellite images and geological data to find sites.

AI doesn't just help with rovers on other planets; it also makes satellites that orbit Earth and other planets smarter. These satellites get a huge amount of data, including very high-resolution pictures and all kinds of environmental measurements. Smart satellites and powerful computer models can do a lot with the data they collect.

AI is going to promote new ideas that will change how we explore space. One big opportunity is to create habitats run by AI for humans going to Mars for a long time. These places would be self-sufficient and manage everything needed to keep humans safe for a long time. On one hand, that's a pretty crazy idea. Could we make habitats there? The Martian environment is extreme. Humans are natural explorers, and going to Mars is what we dream about. We want to live there with our own habitat. And like any scientist in the solar system, we want to find life or at least see where it used to be.

Now, international space exploration shows how humans can work together. From the first joint U.S.-Soviet mission in 1975 to today's work with over fifteen space agencies from different nations, space explorers make the most of cooperating. But, international cooperation on the ground or in space has challenges and many moving parts. That's where AI can help. AI can assist with the collaborations needed to make these missions successful by improving planning, coordination, information sharing, and problem-solving among the many people and agencies involved. AI could work much like the human mission control centers do now.

Artificial intelligence is pushing space exploration into a new era by giving us new tools and new capabilities to move beyond our own planet. The potential uses and opportunities are almost limitless. AI is not just helping to explore more fully and understand more deeply the planets in our solar system and the stunning diversity of moons around them; its use in studying satellite data here on Earth promises a future of discovery that expands our knowledge dramatically.

10

AI IN HEALTHCARE

Think about going into a doctor's office and getting almost instant results from your X-rays. An AI system that has seen millions of medical images provides the feedback. This future is here now, and it's changing healthcare, making it faster and more precise. AI is reshaping the medical field in ways that go beyond just improving diagnostics. Let's take a look at some of the biggest changes.

AI IN MEDICAL IMAGING: ENHANCING ACCURACY

AI is helping us understand what's going on inside the body by looking at medical images. Imagine a computer that doesn't just look at X-rays or MRIs but actually interprets them. It helps radiologists find problems and does it with amazing precision.

Why is that possible? Because AI systems, trained on huge datasets of medical images, have learned to see even the tiniest details that might signal trouble. Now, they are looking for those details as possible signs of diseases, especially cancers, which don't show any outside symptoms.

The things we see in today's medical images are often tiny and hard to find. That's why doctors need lots of experience and training to do it right. Now, what if we built a supersmart computer that could help radiologists at least point out the parts of an MRI, CT scan, or X-ray that might show a health problem? What if this computer, using advanced machine learning, could do this with better accuracy and speed than any human? That's pretty much what we're doing.

There are many benefits when it comes to using AI in medical imaging. First of all, it helps cut down on diagnostic mistakes. The machines are finding disease signs much sooner than humans can; sometimes, we're not figuring it out until it's too late to treat the disease effectively. Also, the machines are doing this at lightning speed, which is so important during emergencies. Of course, the best thing would be for humans to have the same kind of accuracy and speed. But even when AI is involved, there's a chance humans can use their judgment to avoid mistakes (diagnostic errors).

Also, AI gives the same results every time. Human radiologists might interpret the same image differently depending on their experience or even how tired they are. But AI gives reliable answers whenever it is used. This trust in consistent results helps us have better trust in medical diagnoses.

Many diagnostic tools that use AI are already being used. For example, **Google DeepMind** has made an AI system that finds eye diseases just by looking at retinal scans. This system saw something it was trained to find and caught it early. It gave us the time we needed to stop something that could have turned serious if it had been left untreated. Another tool made by a different company called **Aidoc** also uses AI to help real doctors make faster decisions with medical images. The people making these tools claim they save lives—but only if we assume that the lives saved by the AI tools are more important than the lives of the people who might have died if they hadn't gotten the care they received.

However, putting AI in medical imaging has some problems. One big problem is getting good data to train it. AI systems need data integrity that is consistent and standardized. They also need this data to show different groups of Asian people. If not, the AI might not work well for everyone. In healthcare, we need to collect and keep these datasets like they're super valuable because they are.

An AI tool that fits a doctor's workflow could revolutionize medicine, but that's a big "if." AI promises to change healthcare, but it has to work within the existing healthcare system, which is often not straightforward. Even simple AI tasks can be hard. A successful healthcare AI needs to do things doctors can't, but smarter, and do them in the same amount of time a doctor would spend on them.

Case Study: AI in Action

Imagine a hospital that uses the AI system from **Aidoc** to help with CT scans done in the emergency room. One day, a patient comes in with obvious signs of a stroke. The AI quickly analyzes the emergency CT scan and finds something that would make any experienced doctor stop and think. There's a blockage in the blood vessels leading to the front part of the brain. Because the AI works so fast, the doctors can begin treatment that might just save the patient's life or at least prevent them from suffering too much.

AI is changing medical imaging, and it's clear that these changes are big and important. The main thing AI is making better is helping doctors figure out what's wrong with patients, usually in images of their bodies. AI definitely isn't replacing radiologists, but it might help some radiologists do more work faster and more accurately. Also, AI could help more doctors who don't specialize in imaging give faster and more accurate diagnoses.

AI IN DRUG DISCOVERY: SPEEDING UP THE PROCESS

Finding new drugs the old way is a long and expensive trip that often lasts more than ten years. It starts by picking a target that, if it's a protein, has to be related to a disease. Then, thousands of possible drugs are tested, many of which never reach patients who need them. Overall, it's a process that can give hope.

AI is a new revolution in drug development, and it uses speed to change how we find new medicines. One of the best things AI can do is figure out quickly (and usually accurately) which compounds will work against a certain target in a disease. Once we find something that looks like a target, we can learn more about it using AI.

When we use AI in early drug discovery, we help researchers with the first part of the three-step process they follow when they find a new drug. This first part is kind of like speed dating—AI helps find the most promising candidates and helps the researchers choose who they'll date (or screen) over the next few weeks or months.

AI is also good at figuring out how well a drug will work and if it will be safe. It looks at huge, complicated sets of data, like how animals and humans react to it, to find patterns we might not see. The most advanced AIs are good at pattern finding. They might even be better than us. So, they get their insights from the data without using our human creativity or intuition. Still, what they predict is happening is mostly from our previous drug discoveries. AI can do things we can't, but it isn't better at doing what we do.

Many companies are now doing important work in AI drug discovery. **Atomwise** uses AI to predict how well a drug will bind to its target, which is a key part of its effectiveness. This technology has already been used to identify promising treatments for several diseases, including Ebola. **Insilico Medicine** uses AI to find new drug targets, which are molecules or pathways in the body that a drug can interact with. It has discovered some new potential treatments for cancer and other diseases.

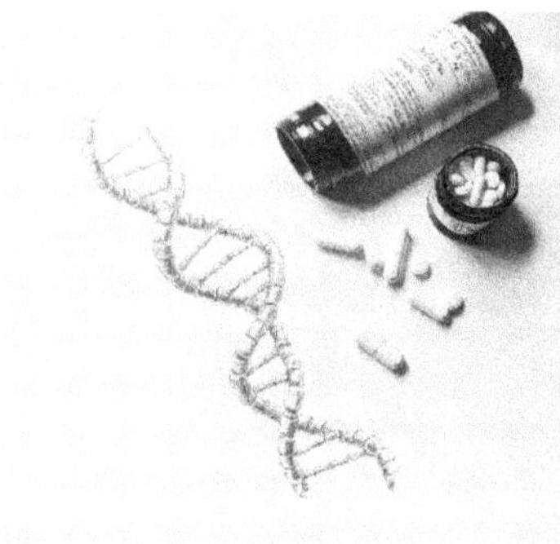

AI is actually making personalized medicine happen for real. The goal of personalized medicine is to customize treatments for each patient according to their genetic makeup and other factors. AI is great at analyzing the huge amounts of genetic data we have now, and it can find patterns that link a person's genes to how they will respond to a specific drug. Then, it tells doctors which treatment to choose. This method, which is almost the opposite of "one size fits all," makes medicine more efficient and effective.

Case Study: Personalized Cancer Therapy

An example of AI in personalized medicine is cancer treatment. AI helps doctors understand how unique genetic changes in each patient's cancer affect tumor growth and the cancer's spread. These insights help doctors choose therapies that target the tumor's particular weaknesses. Overall, cancer care has improved, and many patients are living longer because of this.

In short, AI is making big changes in drug discovery. It's speeding up the process, cutting costs, and making it more personalized. AI is helping find the best candidates, accurately predict their risks and rewards, and develop drugs that are custom-made for each patient. As AI keeps advancing, it promises to deliver better results and bring real change to healthcare.

11

AI IN SECURITY AND PRIVACY

Picture this: You wake up one morning and find that your bank account has been completely emptied. Not only that, but a hacker has stolen your personal information and broken into your email like they were in a spy movie. As more and more people store their lives online, from social media to banking, one thing is becoming very clear: We need strong cybersecurity, not just for ourselves but for everyone in the digital world. Overall, the situation isn't getting better. Cyberattacks are happening more often and affecting more people. However, there's a new tool to help in this digital war: artificial intelligence.

AI IN CYBERSECURITY: PROTECTING YOUR DATA

Cybersecurity is getting better because of AI. The way we protect our sensitive data is changing. Rules and patterns we used to rely on are outdated. AI can do things we couldn't even imagine before. These are things people just can't do as fast or well. AI can look through lots of data. It finds signs of attacks happening right now or about to happen. AI finds these signs better than any human ever could. AI helps us deal with a big problem in cybersecurity. The problem is that we don't have enough skilled people, and the work we have to do just keeps growing.

AI can do lots of smart things in cybersecurity. It can spot strange patterns in network data or traffic. It works because AI can look at huge amounts of data fast. So, when a strange pattern pops up, the AI already knows how things usually look. For example, let's say an AI system handles 60 million requests every second. At real-time speed (which is always debatable in computers), that's about 3,600 trillion operations every minute.

Based on past data, machine learning models predict possible future security breaches. We use these models to find signals that might show a threat is on the way. They look at what's happened before to spot patterns and changes. If we can see cyberattacks coming, we can stop them. This is a big "if," though. It's not as easy as picking and using the right machine-learning methods correctly. To get good results, we need the right data, a smart way to think about the problem, and a clear understanding of how the patterns the ML finds relate to what's happening.

When it comes to finds missed, AI shines. It's not just that experts make good choices. It's also because AI spots patterns that people can't see right away. A great example of this is how antivirus programs have changed. The old ones found viruses by their signatures.

If the program didn't find a signature, it assumed the file was okay.

Now, many programs use AI. They look at how files behave. They ask questions like: "Is this file doing something strange? Is it acting like a virus would?"

AI's use in finding and stopping zero-day exploits shows how effective it can be. These kinds of attacks hit software flaws that antivirus programs can't find because they aren't set up for them. They are like surprises. But AI can use its almost magical powers of prediction to spot them. It can do this by watching how files, including the ones being attacked, behave in strange ways, both before and during the attack. For example, a company called **Cylance** has never been proven wrong after it predicted an antivirus program would. Cylance does this because it has a level of insight and ability that antivirus programs, which work only after the fact, can't match.

AI is also affecting how we log in and who can access what, which are key security areas. The last few years have seen a wave of biometric access controls being made almost everywhere, like on smartphones. The most popular methods seem to be fingerprint scanning and facial recognition. I think the main reason AI is used in these systems is because of its power in machine learning.

Totally guessing here, but I think that's because biometric authentication is a classic "feature and pattern recognition" problem. You need to recognize a person's unique traits (a "feature") in real time for the access control to work. Also, AI biometrics seems to "know" the important features on someone's face or the ridges of their fingerprint.

Another AI invention is **adaptive authentication**, which is used to improve security. It works by examining how users normally act. Most security systems are pretty rigid. They check if users are who they say they are. They do this by looking at things like passwords or security questions. Some systems have gone further. They've added methods like fingerprint recognition. However, the best systems change how they work based on who is using them and how they are using them. This means they raise or lower security risks based on user behavior. They set a normal level and then check how much users differ from it.

Phishing is still one of the easiest and most effective ways for cybercriminals to get sensitive information from people. But at the same time, artificial intelligence (AI) is helping us find and stop these threats. The newest AI, especially natural language processing (NLP), is good at understanding human language. It lets us filter and analyze the huge number of emails sent every day. In fact, we receive about 107 trillion emails every year. For example, an NLP model looks for phishing emails by checking the strange words, phrases, and structures that real ones don't have. At the same time, another AI program checks for fake websites by looking at things like how it is set up, their SSL (secure sockets layer) certificate, and their domain age to see if it is an actual phishing site. When these two programs work together, they give us a much higher chance of spotting phishing scams early and avoiding serious two-way communications.

Phishing Detection Checklist

Here's a handy list to help you spot phishing scams:

1. **Check the sender.** Look for strange differences in the email address or spelling mistakes. Is it from someone you know?
2. **Check links.** Move your mouse over links to see the real URL before you click. If the domain name doesn't match, be suspicious.
3. **Check for urgency.** It means looking for emails that say you need to do something now. Scammers often trick you by making you think there's an emergency. They want you to act fast so you don't notice their lies.
4. **Look at the language.** Check for bad grammar or strange wording that might show this is a phishing scam.

5. **Look over the attachments**. Don't open attachments from people you don't know. First, scan them with antivirus software.

If you get a surprise request for personal information, call the organization directly using a phone number you trust. Then, you can ask if the request was real.

You can safeguard yourself from phishing attacks and keep your personal info safe by following these tips.

Some phishing messages might look harmless or even friendly. But any email, text, or message that tries to get your private info is a phishing attempt.

AI is making huge advances. It now plays an important role in cybersecurity. It can not only find threats but also stop them. AI can do many things. It can make user authentication better and reduce phishing attacks. Phishing is when attackers try to steal passwords. AI is helpful because it works faster and smarter than humans. AI can help us stay one step ahead of cyber enemies who never sleep.

BALANCING AI INNOVATION WITH PRIVACY CONCERNS

Finding a way to manage AI's ethical problems while also protecting individual privacy is a tough but important task. AI systems need huge amounts of data to work well. This big need creates a kind of friction, or perhaps even an ethical dilemma, between the good things AI can bring and the right to privacy. On one hand, collecting lots of data makes AI more accurate and efficient. On the other, we have to think about things like consent, data ownership, and AI's powerful ability to "see" when it's linked up with other technologies, like facial recognition. Ethical questions pop up everywhere you look. And when you consider that AI is being used in surveillance systems that can watch public spaces, follow people, and gather data without asking first, these ethical questions get even more serious.

To deal with people's privacy worries, new AI methods that protect user information are being created. One of these methods is called **federated learning**. In federated learning, many smart devices work together to train a single AI model. Instructions for training the model are sent to the devices. The devices then send back their answers. Think of it like an AI training camp where the "trainees" are the smart devices. The smart devices do their part to train the AI model, but they don't share any of the raw data they used during training. This keeps sensitive user information private.

Differential privacy is a promising technique. It guarantees that during analysis, single data points stay protected from being identified. This method allows researchers to learn from large amounts of data while keeping the privacy of individuals whose data is included in the set. In other words, differential privacy lets us answer big-picture questions about a population without ever exposing any part of it. It does this by adding a clever type of "noise" to the data itself or to the conclusions drawn from it. The funny kind of noise works like this: It makes the result unclear enough that you can't reliably link it to any one person in the dataset yet clear enough that it remains useful for understanding the general trend.

Following regulatory rules is super important if we want to keep making cool AI while protecting people's privacy. In the EU, the **General Data Protection Regulation (GDPR)** is famous for having very high privacy standards, even though some would say impossibly so. And it affects a lot more than just Europe. Anyone doing business in or with the EU has to follow these rules. And they don't let you use personal data to power AI unless you're very careful and do it the right way, which is exactly how they want it to be.

The **California Consumer Privacy Act (CCPA)** provides protections similar to those of the European Union's General Data Protection Regulation (GDPR). However, the CCPA's rules are clearer and easier to follow. These regulations require AI companies to do three things: **Known Data Collection**. People have the right to know all the ways their data is secretly collected and used. The second rule is about **Requesting Deletion**. California residents can ask companies to delete all the personal data that has been collected about them. The third part is **Data Sale Opt-Out**. Residents can stop AI companies from selling their personal data to other businesses.

Finding a way between AI progress and protecting privacy needs clear plans. One good plan is using "**privacy by design.**" That means we make sure privacy rules apply at every step of AI development. Take the example of developing an AI-powered smart home device. When creating it, you think about privacy from the start, like how it will collect data (maybe from sensors), what data it will use (like voice), and where that data will go and be stored.

Another important strategy is working with stakeholders. A key part of this is making sure the AI systems are made openly and responsibly. To do this, developers should involve users, privacy advocates, and even regulators in the development process. By talking openly with these groups, developers can gain trust and make sure the AI systems are built with different views in mind. For example, a tech company making an AI-powered social media platform might hold public meetings to discuss the project's privacy issues and get community feedback.

It's important to create strong data rules if we want to protect user data. These rules must be clear and strict about how data is collected, stored, and processed. This is about making sure we follow the law. But the rules need something else: People need to understand them and be willing to follow them. They need to be good enough to stand up in court if they ever have to. Making data governance policies a big deal is the best way to make people pay attention. And when people pay attention, they'll do a better job handling data.

To sum up, AI and privacy have complicated ethical issues. But we can get through them if we're careful and take steps to protect people. AI systems can be built in ways that respect privacy. This is kind of like AI being designed for federated learning. AI also works well with a privacy method called differential privacy. Following rules like the GDPR and CCPA is super important if we want to keep people's data safe and trust them. And using good practices, like building systems with privacy in mind, talking to everyone involved, and making strong data governance rules, can help protect privacy in the middle of AI innovation.

12

AI FOR SOCIAL GOOD

Think about a world where technology isn't just for entertainment or making our lives easier but can actually be used to save lives. Innovations in artificial intelligence (AI) are helping us get to that life-saving world. We are saving lives, not just improving our own day-to-day tasks.

An example of how this works: People in New Orleans who lived through Katrina now work with AI experts at the University of Chicago. They use AI to predict tornadoes. Why? Because science can do that, and it's much easier to evacuate a city before a tornado than to try to rescue people after it hits. Scientists have figured out the why and how of tornadoes, down to the details of their paths. So, for many folks in New Orleans, the AI predicting disasters seems like a miracle.

AI IN DISASTER RESPONSE: SAVING LIVES

Predicting natural disasters has improved thanks to artificial intelligence. For example, scientists are using machine learning more and more. Now, this method analyzes huge amounts of historical weather data. They use it to make more accurate predictions. They predict extreme weather events like hurricanes and floods.

AI is good at finding patterns. It sees connections in the data that humans might miss. For example, by looking at sea surface temperatures, wind speeds, and different types of pressure in the atmosphere, AI can predict, with much greater accuracy than traditional methods, which vary in their success, where hurricanes will form and where they will go after they form.

AI is also improving how we predict earthquakes. AI systems look at seismic activity to try to predict future earthquakes. By watching tiny shifts in the Earth's crust, these systems are getting better at finding the warning signs of big earthquakes.

For example, some AI models (most are machine learning models) analyze data from all over the world to predict earthquakes. They also improve risk assessments, helping communities prepare better. And here's something cool: Some AI models tell us when we might have the next "Big One."

AI is helping people prepare for emergencies and disasters. Predictions are always the first and most important thing in disaster risk reduction. If we can guess what might happen in the future, we can reduce the impact on people. AI improves predictions in many ways. It finds relationships and patterns in the past that humans are too slow or not smart enough to see. If we think about what's possible and talk about it a lot, we'll come to the same conclusion that AI does. And sometimes, we'll come to it much faster. Then, AI can use all this data to better predict the future. Overall, AI is making our predictions during emergency and disaster risk reduction much more precise and, importantly, actionable.

AI used to manage rescue operations is one of the most convincing examples of what it can do. AI systems look at social media and other online content to find people who need help. For instance, during the 2017 Mexico City earthquake, AI tools worked with human intuition and empathy. They helped emergency responders find people trapped under fallen buildings. AI worked mostly by processing the huge amount of tweets and other social media posts that got sent out during the quake.

Evaluating damage and planning how to recover after a disaster is important. This is another area where AI shows its strength. Drones with cameras fly over affected places. They take lots of photos that are later stitched together to make a complete image of the area. AI can help determine if buildings are still standing or have been flattened. It can tell if roads are usable or if landslides are blocking them. AI can also find places that need immediate help, like scenes of collapsed buildings or fires that haven't been put out yet.

AI can use big data to figure out what will happen when disasters like earthquakes and floods hit. These predictions tell us how bad the damage will be. We get this info from the AI models' simulations. These models look at the most recent data about the disaster and the area it will affect. They also use data from past disasters. By doing this, they come up with forecasts that are often much more detailed and pretty accurate. Communities can use these predictions when they talk about resilience with their gamble.

Case Study: AI in Disaster Response

AI has helped disaster response a lot, and we can see that clearly in what happened with Cyclone Idai in Mozambique in 2019. AI systems were used to warn people about the cyclone. They detected it and predicted where it would go. This gave the government time to evacuate many people from areas directly in its path. The systems also helped with disaster coordination afterward.

AI has been used in **Facebook's Meta Platforms** to predict where new deadly diseases will show up and in the military to predict where enemy attacks will happen.

In the 2017 Mexico City earthquake, another AI experiment showed how effective it could be in emergencies. The Red Cross always has people on the ground waiting to help during disasters. Their volunteers spent years getting trained to work in difficult conditions. But, the Red Cross also uses technology to find the needy. During the quake, their staff used Twitter. The AI tool looking at Twitter helped them find people in trouble. When buildings collapsed, it showed where they were. The Twitter tool was used to rescue people who were buried alive under debris.

Using AI to help people during disasters shows how powerful AI can be for social good. For example, if we can predict a disaster like an earthquake or tsunami well enough, we might be able to give people warnings that let them save their lives and the lives of others.

AI IN EDUCATION FOR UNDERSERVED COMMUNITIES

Think about a student in a poor village who never had an opportunity to learn like kids in rich, modern cities. Even though their fundamental human rights aren't being respected, something amazing is happening thanks to advancements in technology and artificial intelligence. This village student is suddenly getting the same or close to the same level of high-quality education AI promises to give to every kid in the world. Actually, AI is already bridging the education gap between the wealthy and the poor, isn't it?

Adaptive learning systems personalize the learning experience even more. They look at how a student is doing right now, and they spot strengths and weaknesses almost instantly. Then, they change what the student learns and how he or she learns it. Sometimes, they make it easier; sometimes they make it harder. They do this to give exactly the kind of help (or challenge) that each student needs.

Education is often limited by language, especially in communities where many languages are spoken. Students who can't understand their teachers' words struggle to learn. Things have changed; now, software developers have created AI-powered translation tools to help students understand. When these tools aren't around, students can't understand the lesson. If they don't understand the lesson, they can't succeed in school. Tools like speech recognition, which turns speech into text, and text-to-speech, which turns text into speech, help students with disabilities. They make sure these students can participate in lessons. AI also helps by making sure students can hear everything the teacher says.

Teachers working in underserved communities face many challenges. They often have limited resources and few opportunities to grow. But AI is here to help. AI tools offer development programs that act like pretend teaching assistants. They give teachers much-needed resources and some feedback they can use right away. Plus, AI looks into teacher-student interactions in a way no human can. It helps figure out what's working in class and what's not. For example, an AI tool might notice that a whole class is getting the same topic wrong. Then, it tells the teacher: "Fix that problem and think about how you can explain it differently."

AI systems can help teachers in remote places where there aren't many professional development opportunities. Even in these areas, teachers can use AI systems to get quick access to the latest teaching resources and expert advice. Teachers in underserved communities can use AI to improve themselves and become better versions of the educators society needs. These systems are good at suggesting ways to use different, promising, but not yet widely used teaching methods. They offer persistent, sometimes annoying, nudges to try new things. They also help teachers talk and work together more, even when they are physically separated from their colleagues.

Case Study: AI Tutors in Rural India

AI tutors are changing the learning game in rural India, where kids have very few opportunities to get a good education. Some people might think that getting access to something as high-tech as artificial intelligence would be impossible. But these smart AI systems are actually doing something very important—helping students catch up with friends in the city and making real progress in the education system. These rural kids aren't just reducing the big gap in access to good education between them and city kids; they're doing it in a way that seems almost miraculous.

AI has a huge opportunity to help fix the gaps in education we see today. It can provide amazing opportunities for whole communities that have been left out for much too long. And it can make learning more personal and better for the people who need it the most. Students in underfunded schools do not only deserve the best resources available to them. They also deserve the kind of teaching that connects with them deeply and supports their growth. This is a level of care that I'm not sure many of us would say they get from most teachers right now.

AI IN PUBLIC HEALTH INITIATIVES

Imagine a world where health disasters are discovered and fixed before they get bad. That's what AI can do for public health. Machine learning models don't just look at medical data; they listen to us. Yep, they check what we say online. It turns out that when lots of us say something at the same time, it means more than you might think. The word is "semaphore." If you don't know, semaphore is a system of signals. It was invented in the early 1800s. People used it to send messages over long distances. When they couldn't use words, they'd wave flags around.

The part of AI where it helps with public health also includes teaching people about health and making them aware of health issues. Now, AI chatbots are used in ways we never thought of before. They are giving out reliable health information. They work like health advisors, twenty-four hours a day, seven days a week. They are answering the many health questions people ask during these unusual times. And when I say these unusual times, I'm talking about the starting phase of what we now call the COVID-19 pandemic.

Many areas where people live and work are not served well by healthcare, and this is a huge challenge. Access to medical help is limited, and sometimes, there are good reasons for this. AI is helping solve the problems of limited access and traveling long distances. The first way we're using AI to help isn't about the AI itself. Telemedicine isn't new, but using AI can make follow-up calls more efficient. AI can also improve outcomes by better triaging who needs to be seen and who can continue talking with a chatbot.

Case Study: AI in Public Health

The **Centers for Disease Control (CDC)** uses artificial intelligence to monitor and respond to flu outbreaks. These AI systems look at lots of different data. They use their algorithms to track how the flu is moving. By spotting potential outbreaks ahead of time, the CDC can use its resources better and, hopefully, stop the flu from spreading. Another example comes from a group called **Hurdle**, which helps mental health in underserved communities. Hurdle uses AI to figure out which people are probably at risk for mental health issues. Then, it reaches out to these people with support and resources.

AI is helping public health in a big way. The tools we have now, and the ones we're making for the future, help us understand and solve health problems better. This is better and faster than what we could do before. AI predicts where diseases will spread. It finds the next big health risk coming. That could be a new germ or something else. It describes how these threats affect different parts of our population.

13

AI IN FINANCE

Imagine getting a nice morning message on your phone: "Good morning! Based on how you've been spending this month, we've made some changes. Your dining-out and entertainment budget has been adjusted. You saved an extra $50 compared to last month!" This is AI in personal finance, helping us handle our money better with almost no effort. AI tools are changing what personal finance means. They're giving us new, smarter, and sometimes even sharper ways to budget, plan, and manage our debts.

AI IN PERSONAL FINANCE: MANAGING YOUR MONEY

People like how AI is taking over budgeting tools. These tools offer insight and precision we could hardly imagine a few years ago. But AI and personal finance aren't new ideas joined together. **Mint**, the budgeting app, launched back in 2006 was not a smart app then, but now it uses AI to help people be more aware of their spending habits.

AI is a helpful partner for long-term planning. For example, the company called **Wealthfront** has people and AI that give you truly personalized financial advice. Wealthfront looks at your age, income, how much risk you can handle, and your financial goals. Then it makes investment plans for you that are one of a kind.

And that's not all. Wealthfront also does super smart things with your retirement planning and future projections. The AI behind its "calculators" is very advanced and gives you lots of powerful ways to think inside and outside the box.

Another area where AI is making a big difference is managing debts. That's because AI is awesome at practical problem-solving. It finds the best and most efficient ways to reach a goal. And paying off debts is a classic problem where you want to find the fastest way to get to zero. Apps like **Tally** can help you solve this problem. They use AI to organize your debts and give you clear steps to follow. Tally even adjusts its advice based on your behavior, showing you the paths (solutions) you seem most likely to take (follow).

AI-driven apps offer a simple way to understand your spending habits. They connect to your bank accounts and credit cards, so they can check your spending live right on the app. We can see what we're spending on almost instantly. But what if we could use AI to do more with our money, not just check how much we're spending? What if we could plan better for the money we might spend later?

Interactive Element: Personal Finance Checklist

Here are some basic steps to get started with using AI for managing your money:

1. **Download a budgeting app**. Pick a budgeting app that has AI features. Good choices are **Mint** or **YNAB (You Need A Budget)**.
2. **Set up your profile**. Make a profile and enter your basic details like income, how much you want to save, and where you usually spend money.
3. **Track your spending**. Start keeping track of your spending. It's best if you can connect the app to your bank accounts and credit cards.
4. **Check your budget.** Look at the app's budget suggestions regularly and see how it's doing with your goals.
5. **Make a plan.** Use **Wealthfront** or another app to make a financial plan for your future. This includes saving for retirement and building wealth over time.
6. **Pay off debt.** Find ways to automate and speed up your debt payments, especially with credit cards.
7. **Watch your spending**. Pay attention to how you're spending money and keep yourself in check.

AI IN FRAUD DETECTION: KEEPING YOUR MONEY SAFE

Picture yourself opening your bank account online and seeing transactions you never approved. This creepy experience happens to many people. But we can stop it. AI is the main reason why. Its real-time data monitoring skills are unmatched by anything else. In the "old days," banks would notice fraud after it happened. That's when customers reported missing money. Now, with AI's help, many fraud cases are spotted before anyone loses anything. AI sees things we humans often miss, like two transactions for $500 each that suddenly pop up in our account, along with six other strange transfers.

AI has been very successful at stopping credit card fraud. AI systems keep watching transactions all the time, looking for strange spending. For example, if someone suddenly starts using a credit card in a foreign country while the card owner is at home, an AI system will mark this as suspicious. **FICO Falcon** is one of the top tools that banks use to find credit card fraud. **FICO Falcon** works with the bank's AI system. It uses past data to create a "normal" spending pattern for each card. Then, it looks for times when someone's spending pattern isn't normal.

There's another worry called identity theft that keeps getting worse, and AI is helping us deal with it. AI algorithms are super good at spotting possible identity theft. They do this by keeping an almost constant watch on us and our digital habits. They notice the smallest changes in how we act online and then alert the people who need to know. Most of the time, we're totally unaware of our "twin" AI that's always watching over us. But what happens when our digital doppelganger (made by AI) isn't around? Or, even scarier, when AI starts doing eavesdropping for someone else? Well, that's a dark topic for another day.

AI is an effective tool against money laundering. Banks and other financial companies use AI to look at transactions and find out if they are clean or connected to crime. AI can find the right clues over and over again, usually better than humans can. Many of these clues can only be found using the advanced math that most of us would call "figuring it out." AI works silently behind the scenes and is very good at spotting the unusual patterns that criminals use to hide their actions.

Why is using AI (which means machine learning, ML, after the math) connected to making money laundering schemes look normal so important? Because it's the main way we have right now to find and follow the invisible paths that criminals use.

Interactive Element: Fraud Detection Checklist

Here are some tips to help you avoid fraud and stay secure:

1. **Always check your accounts.** Look at your bank and credit card statements regularly. Fraud is often caught early by people who notice strange charges and check things out.
2. **Make it harder for fraudsters.** Setting up alerts is a simple way to add another layer of protection. This way, you'll be warned if someone tries to use your accounts without permission.
3. **Use what you already have.** Most of the time, using biometric authentication (like face ID or fingerprints) is just as safe as logging in with a password.
4. **Check for unusual actions.** If you get an alert (or notice something yourself) and think it might be fraud, don't just dismiss it. Take two minutes to check it out with your bank.
5. **Understand how to use the security features.** With everything online now, it's up to you to set up the security features your bank offers.

14

AI IN RETAIL

Imagine the perfect shopping experience. You go to your favorite store, and it has exactly what you want every time. For many people, this is a kind of retail paradise. But making it happen wouldn't be possible without today's advanced AI inventory systems turning it from a dream into a reality. That's what the National Retail Federation told us; we also got this info from other business experts and magazines. When it comes to stocking stores, possible solutions are mixed with real problems. Finding the right balance is crucial for companies. Too much stock isn't good, and too little can be a disaster.

AI IN INVENTORY MANAGEMENT: EFFICIENCY AND ACCURACY

AI makes inventory management more efficient and accurate, especially when trying to predict customer demand. By looking at past sales data, machine learning models can find patterns and trends that might be too complicated for humans to see. These models analyze many factors, including past sales, to make their predictions. For example, Walmart uses AI to analyze data from stores all over the world. Its AI includes factors like holidays, weather, and local events to predict which products will be in high demand at stores in different areas. This kind of precision not only improves customer satisfaction but also helps reduce the costs that come from having too much stock or not enough stock.

AI also helps with managing inventory. Regular inventory management often needs people to count things. That method is too slow and not reliable enough for many stores. They can't use it to track thousands of items. Some big retailers, like Walmart and Target, have warehouse systems that work well. But even those systems can't guarantee that a needed item is in the right store. AI can figure out, maybe more accurately than humans, what items will be used quickly and which ones will be used slowly. That way, AI helps stores get the right amount of every item. Then, stores can use IoT devices to keep checking. They make sure all the items stay where they're supposed to be.

AI can now automate the restocking process to keep inventory levels exactly where they should be. These AI systems watch how much stock is left and reorder items when they drop below a certain level. Many of them are linked to supplier networks, allowing for smooth and often seamless restocking. When they place orders, they usually do it in waves to reduce costs. We never see grocery store managers doing large-scale cash handovers to suppliers. That's because AI-driven supply chain systems are designed to avoid big spending surprises.

One huge advantage of AI in inventory management is that it can optimize inventory across several different locations. For example, in a recent study by McKinsey & Company, an unnamed North American retailer used AI to find the best ways to distribute inventory for one hundred different products across fifty locations. Predictive analytics (also known as predictive modeling) are used to make forecasts. They are often used in inventory management to predict future demands so retailers can stock enough of each product but not too much. If stock levels are optimized, each location will have enough of the products that should be there to satisfy demand without having too many unwanted items.

Interactive Element: Inventory Management Checklist

The article "How to Use AI for Better Inventory Management" says that retailers are taking a big step by using AI, which will greatly change how efficient their inventory management systems are. The article explains that the efficiency of an inventory system is about how well it can align supply with customer demand. That is, the system should ensure that products are available not just in the "right" places but also at the "right" times. The article also shows how retailers can achieve this by using the six "action steps" recommended by the Harvard Business Review.

AI IN CUSTOMER INSIGHTS: UNDERSTANDING CONSUMER BEHAVIOR

In retail, it's super important to know your customers, and AI has made this a lot easier by giving us better and deeper insights into how customers act. When you go shopping, whether online or in a store, AI is working behind the scenes, looking at your every move. It's checking out not just what you're buying but also what you're looking at (and probably not buying, like me!). It analyzes huge amounts of data to find trends, patterns, and next moves. For example, the algorithms can predict if you're going to buy something again soon and if you might be interested in something else that goes great with it. But it also looks at what you're checking out, all the stuff you do on social media, and the text in reviews and comments.

AI brings lots of benefits to retail, like tailored marketing. You might think it feels awkward when stores suggest products. It's almost like someone is looking over your shoulder. But when stores use AI to offer personalized ads, they seem to "get" you better. These ads aren't just annoying pop-ups. They're smart suggestions for things you might want to buy. If a store doesn't know what to show you, that's a missed opportunity for both you and the store. And, of course, from the store's point of view, the more relevant the ads are, the more likely you are to say, "Yes, I'd like to try that."

AI is awesome for figuring out customer segments. Retailers can't use the same marketing for everyone anymore. AI helps divide customers into different groups based on how they act. Machine learning models look at the data and find these groups. Then, retailers can market to these groups differently. For example, high-value customers could be treated like VIPs and get exclusive offers and first access to new products. Other customers might get a little more money-off promotion to get them to spend more often. If "one-to-few" is the goal for retailers, being "one-to-some" is pretty good too. AI makes it easier to reach both goals effectively.

Improving the shopping experience is definitely the biggest benefit of AI, and that's what people notice the most. Cheaper and more powerful computing has made AI chatbots common. These chatbots offer 24/7 customer service, answering questions, handling orders, and doing everything from A to Z in the buying process. They are basically the perfect customer service helpers we've always wanted. AI also gives us product recommendations, both online and in the stores. In the store, a sales associate might suggest something you didn't think of on your own and say, "You should try this." AI can do that for many more customers, making their shopping experience smoother and more enjoyable. At Nordstrom, both in-store and online experiences are enhanced by AI. In-store sales associates use data to recommend items that align with customer preferences. Online, AI helps customers find what they are looking for and discover new products that match their tastes.

In retail, AI is totally changing the way we understand customers. Its huge amounts of data and the amazing insights that come from it are quickly making AI the most important tool for understanding today's complicated and always-changing shoppers.

These efficiency-gaining advancements create a more engaging and satisfying experience for customers. But how are they affecting the job market? Let's start with the new opportunities AI is creating. Then, we'll talk about job displacement, which is the main concern people have about AI taking over.

15

AI IN COMMUNICATION

Imagine having a conversation with someone from another country, despite not speaking their language, and yet understanding each other perfectly. This isn't a futuristic dream but a current reality, thanks to AI-powered language translation. AI can bridge linguistic gaps, making communication among people with no formal language training understandable to each other. This chapter explores how AI has revolutionized language translation, making global communication more accessible than ever.

AI IN LANGUAGE TRANSLATION: BRIDGING GLOBAL GAPS

The evolution of AI in language translation has been truly remarkable. Initially, language translation depended on rule-based systems, which used predefined linguistic rules and dictionaries. While groundbreaking at the time, these systems often resulted in awkward and inaccurate translations. The advent of **statistical machine translation (SMT)** marked a significant improvement in analyzing large sets of bilingual text to predict translations. SMT increased accuracy but still struggled with context and idiomatic expressions.

The introduction of **neural machine translation (NMT)** was a game-changer. Unlike its predecessors, NMT uses deep learning to model entire sentences as sequences, allowing it to understand the context and nuances of language. This results in translations that are more fluent and natural. NMT systems are trained on extensive datasets, learning the subtleties of languages, idioms, and cultural references. This shift from rule-based and statistical methods to neural networks has vastly improved translation quality and reliability.

Today, AI-powered translation tools are essential in our interconnected world. **Google Translate** is a prime example, offering real-time translation for over one hundred languages. Whether you're traveling or conversing with someone who speaks a different language, Google Translate can instantly translate text, speech, and even images containing foreign text. This tool has democratized access to translation, making it available to anyone with an internet connection.

Another outstanding tool is **DeepL**, which is known for its high-quality translations. DeepL excels in understanding context and producing translations that sound natural. It uses advanced neural networks trained on diverse texts, allowing it to capture the nuances of different languages. DeepL's contextual understanding often surpasses that of other translation tools, making it a favorite among professional translators and businesses.

Microsoft Translator also stands out with its integration into various Microsoft services. It offers real-time translation for text, voice, and images and integrates smoothly with tools like **Microsoft Office** and **Teams**. This integration is especially valuable for businesses operating internationally, allowing employees to collaborate across language barriers effortlessly.

AI facilitates real-time translation, enabling instant communication across different languages. AI-powered speech-to-text and text-to-speech technologies enable live translations during conversations, speeches, and meetings. For example, during international business meetings, AI-driven devices can translate spoken language in real time, allowing participants to understand each other without needing a human interpreter. These technologies not only translate words but also capture tone and intent, making communication more effective.

Real-time translation devices and applications are becoming increasingly popular. Handheld gadgets or smartphone apps can translate conversations on the fly, which is especially useful for travelers. Devices like **Pocketalk** and **Travis Touch** offer instant translation in multiple languages, making travel more convenient and enjoyable.

AI also supports multilingual communication in various contexts. AI chatbots, for instance, provide customer support in multiple languages. They can understand and respond to queries in different languages, ensuring a consistent customer experience regardless of linguistic background. This capability is invaluable for global companies seeking to provide seamless support to their diverse customer base.

Language learning apps driven by AI are another significant advancement. Apps like **Duolingo** use AI to create personalized learning experiences. Duolingo's AI-powered platform adapts lessons based on user progress and areas of difficulty, ensuring an engaging and effective learning process. The app also uses speech recognition to help users practice pronunciation, making language learning more interactive and practical.

The advancements in AI translation technologies have indeed bridged global gaps, enabling people from different linguistic backgrounds to connect and communicate effortlessly. The shift from rule-based systems to neural networks has revolutionized translation accuracy and fluency. Tools like Google Translate, DeepL, and Microsoft Translator showcase the power of AI in making translation accessible to everyone. Real-time translation devices and applications facilitate instant conversation across languages, while AI-driven chatbots and language learning apps enhance multilingual communication and education.

Reflection Section: Consider Your Language Translation Needs

1. **Personal Use:** Reflect on situations where AI translation tools could benefit you. How might they simplify your travel experiences or help you communicate with friends and family who speak different languages?
2. **Professional Use:** Consider how AI-powered translation could improve your work, especially if you operate in an international or multicultural environment. How could tools like Microsoft Translator or DeepL enhance your productivity and collaboration with colleagues?
3. **Learning Opportunities:** Think about the potential of AI-driven language learning apps. If you've ever wanted to learn a new language, how might an app like Duolingo make the process more engaging and effective for you?

AI IN SOCIAL MEDIA: PERSONALIZING CONTENT

Social media has become a central part of our daily lives, and AI plays a crucial role in shaping our experiences on these platforms. One of the most significant ways AI enhances social media is through content recommendation. AI algorithms analyze user behavior to suggest content that is most likely to engage or interest you. These algorithms track your interactions, such as the posts you like, share, or comment on and the time you spend on various types of content. By understanding your preferences and habits, AI curates a personalized news feed tailored to

your interests. For example, **Facebook** uses sophisticated AI algorithms to curate its news feed, considering factors like your past interactions, the popularity of posts among your friends, and even the time of day to present content that is most relevant to you. This personalization keeps you engaged, ensuring that you see the most interesting and pertinent posts whenever you log in.

AI also plays a vital role in social media analytics, providing insights into user engagement and trends. **Natural language processing (NLP)** is a key technology in this area. NLP analyzes social media posts to gauge sentiment, helping brands understand how their audiences feel about their products or services. For example, an AI tool might analyze tweets about a new product launch to determine whether the sentiment is positive, negative, or neutral. This information is invaluable for marketers aiming to gauge public opinion in real time. AI tools also track hashtags and trending topics, offering a snapshot of what's currently popular or gaining traction. By monitoring these trends, businesses can tailor their marketing strategies to align with the current interests and concerns of their target audience. For instance, a brand might use AI-driven social media analytics to monitor the performance of a campaign, adjusting its strategies based on real-time feedback and engagement metrics. This level of insight allows for more effective and responsive marketing efforts.

Content creation and moderation on social media are other areas where AI proves invaluable. AI can generate content for social media posts and advertisements, making it easier for brands to maintain a consistent and engaging online presence. For example, AI can craft catchy headlines, suggest relevant hashtags, or even create entire posts based on trending topics and user preferences. This automation not only saves time but also ensures that content remains relevant and appealing. On the moderation side, AI algorithms are essential for detecting and removing inappropriate or harmful content. Platforms like **X (formerly Twitter)** use AI to identify and filter out spam, hate speech, and other forms of abusive content. These algorithms scan millions of posts in real time, flagging those that violate community guidelines for further review or automatic removal. This proactive approach helps maintain a safe and positive environment for users, reducing the spread of harmful or misleading information.

AI also enhances user interaction and engagement on social media platforms. AI-powered chatbots are increasingly used for real-time customer interaction. These chatbots handle a wide range of tasks, from answering customer queries to providing personalized recommendations. For example, a brand might use an AI chatbot on its Facebook page to assist customers with product information, track orders, or resolve issues. This instant support not only improves customer satisfaction but also frees up human agents to handle more complex inquiries. Personalized user experiences are another area where AI excels. Features like Instagram's Explore page use AI to suggest content based on your interests and interactions. By analyzing your behavior, AI presents a curated selection of posts, videos, and stories that are most likely to appeal to you. This personalized approach keeps you engaged and encourages you to spend more time on the platform.

Snapchat's use of AI filters and lenses is a prime example of how AI enhances user engagement. These filters use machine learning to detect facial features and apply fun effects in real time. Whether it's transforming your appearance with a whimsical filter or adding interactive elements to your snaps, AI makes the experience more enjoyable and engaging. These features not only entertain users but also encourage them to share their creations, driving further engagement on the platform.

16

AI AND ETHICS

Imagine applying for a job where your resume is filtered not by a human but by an AI system that decides your fate. You're confident in your qualifications, yet you never hear back. Later, you discover that the AI system had biases that worked against you. This unsettling scenario is not fiction but a reality for many. The importance of fairness in AI cannot be overstated. As AI becomes more integrated into our lives, ensuring that these systems are fair and just becomes crucial.

THE MORAL IMPERATIVE OF FAIRNESS IN AI

Fairness in AI means creating and using systems that do not discriminate against any individual or group. It's about providing equal opportunities and outcomes across diverse populations. When we talk about fairness in AI, we refer to the ethical responsibility to ensure that these technologies serve everyone equitably.

This involves designing AI systems that make unbiased decisions and deliver benefits without favoritism or prejudice. Fairness is

not just a technical challenge but a moral duty, demanding a commitment to justice and equality in every aspect of AI development.

Bias in AI systems can enter at various stages, often reflecting historical and societal prejudices. One major source of bias is the data used to train AI models. If the data includes biased information, the AI will learn and perpetuate those biases. For example, if historical hiring data favors one gender over another, an AI system trained on this data might continue this trend, leading to gender bias in hiring algorithms. Similarly, facial recognition systems can exhibit racial biases if they are trained on datasets that underrepresent certain racial groups. These biases result in AI systems that perform poorly or unfairly for those groups, reinforcing existing inequalities.

Algorithmic biases can also be introduced during the model development phase. Even well-intentioned developers can inadvertently create biased algorithms if they do not carefully consider how their models might impact different groups. For instance, an algorithm designed to predict recidivism might disproportionately flag individuals from certain racial backgrounds as high risk due to biases in the training data. These biases can have serious consequences, such as unfair treatment in the criminal justice system or discriminatory hiring practices. Addressing these biases is essential to creating fair and equitable AI systems.

Ensuring fairness in AI requires a multi-faceted approach. One effective strategy is to use diverse and representative training datasets. By including a wide range of data points, developers can help ensure that AI systems learn from a balanced and comprehensive set of examples. This reduces the risk of the AI developing biased behaviors. Regular auditing and testing for bias in AI models are also crucial. This involves continuously monitoring AI systems to identify and correct any biases that may emerge over time. Implementing fairness-aware machine learning techniques is another important method. These techniques are specifically designed to detect and mitigate biases, ensuring that AI systems make fair decisions.

IBM has been a leader in promoting fairness in AI. They have developed tools and frameworks to detect and address biases in their AI systems. For example, **IBM's AI Fairness 360** is an open-source toolkit that helps developers identify and mitigate biases in their models. Similarly, **Google's AI Fairness Research** initiative focuses on developing algorithms and techniques to ensure fairness in AI. They conduct extensive research to understand how biases arise and how they can be mitigated. **Microsoft's Fairlearn toolkit** provides resources for assessing and improving fairness in AI models. This toolkit includes metrics and algorithms to help developers evaluate and enhance the fairness of their AI systems.

Interactive Element: Fairness in AI Case Studies

1. **IBM's AI Fairness 360**: Explore how IBM's toolkit helps developers identify and mitigate biases in AI models. It provides metrics and algorithms to ensure that AI systems make fair decisions.
2. **Google's AI Fairness Research**: Learn about Google's initiatives to promote fairness in AI through research and development. They focus on understanding and addressing biases in AI systems.
3. **Microsoft's Fairlearn Toolkit**: Understand how Microsoft's toolkit provides resources for assessing and

improving fairness in AI models. It includes tools for evaluating the fairness of AI systems and making necessary adjustments.

By examining these case studies, you can gain a deeper understanding of the practical steps being taken to ensure fairness in AI. These efforts highlight the importance of actively addressing biases and promoting equity in AI systems.

TRANSPARENCY IN AI: BUILDING TRUST WITH USERS

Imagine using an AI-driven service that significantly impacts your life, such as a mortgage approval system or a medical diagnosis tool. You would naturally want to understand how these systems make decisions that affect you. Transparency in AI is crucial for building trust with users, ensuring they feel confident in the technology's fairness and reliability. When users understand how AI systems work, they are more likely to trust and accept the results. Transparency also holds AI systems accountable, making it easier to identify and correct errors or biases.

However, achieving transparency in AI systems is not without its challenges. One major barrier is the complexity of AI models, especially deep learning networks. These models often operate as "black boxes," making decisions based on intricate patterns in the data that are difficult to explain. This complexity can make it hard for developers to provide clear explanations for how decisions are made. Additionally, proprietary algorithms and trade secrets in commercial AI settings can limit transparency. Companies may be reluctant to disclose the inner workings of their AI systems for fear of losing a competitive edge or exposing sensitive information.

To enhance transparency, various techniques can make AI decisions more interpretable. One such method is the use of **explainable AI (XAI)** techniques. XAI aims to create models that not only provide accurate results but also offer clear, understandable explanations for their decisions. For example, **LIME (Local Interpretable Model-Agnostic Explanations)** and **SHAP (SHapley Additive exPlanations)** are popular XAI tools. LIME approximates complex models with simpler, interpretable ones, providing insights into how specific decisions are made. SHAP assigns importance values to each feature in a dataset, explaining the influence of each feature on the model's output.

Providing users with clear documentation and explanations of AI processes is another essential step toward transparency. This documentation should include details about the data used to train the model, the algorithms employed, and the decision-making process. By offering comprehensive documentation, developers can help users understand the AI system's capabilities and limitations, fostering trust and confidence. Moreover, involving users in the development process and seeking their feedback can ensure that the explanations provided are relevant and understandable.

Real-world examples of transparent AI systems demonstrate the feasibility and benefits of these approaches. The **Defense Department Advanced Research Projects Agency (DARPA)'s Explainable AI (XAI)** program is a notable initiative aimed at creating AI systems that offer clear, interpretable explanations for their decisions. This program focuses on developing techniques that make AI models more understandable without sacrificing performance. Similarly, **Google's Model Cards** provide clear information about AI models, including their intended use, performance metrics, and potential biases. These cards offer users a comprehensive overview of the AI system, enabling them to make informed decisions about its use.

IBM's AI FactSheets are another excellent example of promoting transparency. These fact sheets detail the capabilities and limitations of AI systems, providing users with a clear understanding of what the AI can and cannot do. By offering this information, IBM helps users set realistic expectations, and fosters trust in their AI technologies. These initiatives highlight the importance of transparency in building trust and ensuring the responsible use of AI.

By focusing on transparency, developers can create AI systems that users trust and understand. This involves overcoming challenges like model complexity and proprietary concerns, using techniques like XAI, and providing clear documentation and examples. By prioritizing transparency, we can build AI systems that are not only powerful but also fair, accountable, and trustworthy.

ACCOUNTABILITY IN AI SYSTEMS

Accountability in AI means ensuring that developers and users are responsible for the outcomes and decisions made by AI systems. It's about establishing clear lines of responsibility for the actions and impacts of AI, whether positive or negative. When an AI system makes a decision, there must be someone who can explain why that decision was made and take responsibility for its consequences. This is especially important in high-stakes areas like healthcare, finance, and criminal justice, where AI decisions can significantly impact people's lives. Accountability ensures that AI systems are developed and used ethically and that there is recourse if something goes wrong.

One of the significant challenges in enforcing accountability is the complexity and opacity of AI decision-making processes. Many AI systems, particularly those using deep learning, operate as "black boxes." They make decisions based on patterns in the data that are not easily interpretable, even by the developers who created them. This lack of transparency makes it difficult to hold anyone accountable when an AI system makes a mistake or causes harm. Additionally, the rapid pace of AI development often outstrips the creation of regulatory frameworks and guidelines, leaving a gap in oversight and enforcement. Without clear regulations, it's challenging to set and maintain standards for accountability.

Robust governance and oversight mechanisms are essential to promoting accountability in AI. This involves setting up structures and processes to monitor AI systems throughout their lifecycle, from development to deployment and beyond. One effective approach is establishing ethical guidelines and best practices for AI development. Organizations like the IEEE have developed frameworks such as **Ethically Aligned Design,** which provides comprehensive guidelines to ensure AI systems are designed and used responsibly. Similarly, the **International Organization for Standardization/International Electrotechnical Commission (ISO/IEC)** standards for AI outline principles and practices for developing accountable AI systems. These frameworks help developers and organizations navigate the ethical complexities of AI and establish clear standards for accountability.

Several real-world examples illustrate how accountability can be ensured in AI systems. The European Union's AI Act is a landmark regulatory framework aimed at ensuring the accountability of AI systems. It sets out requirements for transparency, risk management, and human oversight, particularly for high-risk AI applications. This act holds developers and users accountable for the safe and ethical use of AI, providing a model for other regions to follow. Ethics boards and review committees also play a crucial role in overseeing AI projects. These bodies review AI systems' ethical implications and ensure they meet established standards before deployment.

In the era of ever-increasing autonomous vehicles, accountability becomes even more critical. When an autonomous vehicle is involved in an accident, determining responsibility can be complex. Is it the fault of the vehicle's AI system, the manufacturer, or the software developer? To address these challenges, some jurisdictions have introduced regulations that define clear lines of responsibility. For example, if an autonomous vehicle's AI system fails, the manufacturer might be held accountable, ensuring that there is always a responsible party. This clarity encourages the development of safer and more reliable AI systems, as manufacturers and developers know they will be held accountable for their creations.

Ensuring accountability in AI is not just about preventing harm; it's also about building trust. When users know that there are clear lines of responsibility and that developers are committed to ethical practices, they are more likely to trust and adopt AI technologies. This trust is essential for the widespread acceptance and success of AI. By implementing robust governance mechanisms, establishing ethical guidelines, and learning from real-world examples, we can create AI systems that are not only powerful but also accountable and trustworthy.

17

AI AND CREATIVITY

Imagine watching a movie and discovering that its script was crafted not by a human but by an AI. The dialogues are captivating, the plot is intricate, and the character development is deep. This might sound like science fiction, but it's becoming a reality, shaping the future of film and animation. AI is revolutionizing the entertainment industry, introducing new tools and techniques that boost creativity and streamline production. This chapter explores how AI is breaking new ground in film and animation, offering exciting opportunities for creators and audiences alike.

AI IN FILM AND ANIMATION: NEW FRONTIERS

AI's impact on scriptwriting and story development is one of the most intriguing advancements in the entertainment world. Traditionally, writing a compelling script involves hours of brainstorming, writing, and revising. AI is changing this process by analyzing successful scripts and suggesting plot structures. For example, AI algorithms can review thousands of scripts, identifying common elements that resonate with audiences, such as plot twists, character arcs, and pacing. Tools like **ScriptBook** use predictive analytics to assess script success, helping writers refine their work based on insights from box office hits and critically acclaimed films. This technology offers invaluable feedback for filmmakers, helping them create more engaging and successful stories.

AI goes beyond plot structures by generating dialogue and character interactions. With an understanding of language nuances and context, AI can craft realistic and engaging conversations between characters. This is especially useful in developing story arcs where character development is key. AI can suggest how characters should interact based on their personalities and the story's progression. This not only saves time but also adds depth to the narrative, ensuring characters feel authentic and relatable.

In visual effects (VFX) and animation, AI is making significant strides. Tasks like rotoscoping and compositing, which once required manual tracing over footage, are now being automated by AI. This allows animators to focus on more creative aspects of their work. Machine learning models can create realistic character animations by analyzing motion capture data and applying it to digital models, making characters move naturally and convincingly. **Disney's** use of AI for facial animation in the remake of ***The Lion King*** is a notable example. By employing deep learning algorithms, Disney created highly realistic and expressive animal characters, analyzing human facial expressions and translating them onto animal models. This technology not only improved animation quality but also sped up the production process, achieving high levels of realism more efficiently.

In film editing and post-production, AI has become an essential tool. Editing involves selecting the best scenes, arranging them coherently, and enhancing visual quality. AI tools can automate scene detection and shot selection, making the editing process more efficient. By analyzing the footage, AI can identify key moments and suggest the most impactful shots for the final cut, allowing editors to concentrate on the creative aspects of storytelling rather than tedious tasks. AI-driven software also improves color grading and enhancement. For example, AI can analyze a film's color palette and recommend adjustments to enhance visual appeal, ensuring consistency throughout. **IBM's Watson**, which creates movie trailers by analyzing footage, exemplifies this technology. Watson's AI identifies the most exciting and emotionally charged scenes to craft trailers that capture a film's essence and attract viewers.

AI is also transforming audience engagement and marketing. By analyzing viewing habits and preferences, AI can tailor marketing campaigns to target specific demographics. Personalized recommendations ensure that audiences discover movies and shows that match their interests. For instance, Netflix uses AI to generate personalized thumbnails and trailers based on a viewer's history and preferences. This targeted approach enhances user experience and boosts engagement and viewership.

AI IN GAME DEVELOPMENT: ENHANCING INTERACTIVITY

In game development, AI is more than a tool—it's a driving force behind endless possibilities. Imagine a game where every time you play, the world changes with new landscapes, unique challenges, and fresh storylines. This dynamic experience is made possible through procedural content generation. AI algorithms create infinite levels, terrains, and environments by analyzing patterns and data, producing content that feels handcrafted. For example, ***No Man's Sky*** uses AI to generate a vast universe with billions of planets, each with its own ecosystem. This level of diversity and scale would be unfeasible without AI, as it allows developers to offer players a unique experience every time they play.

AI also transforms the quests and storylines in games. Traditional game development involves manually creating quests and narratives, which can be time-consuming and limit variety. AI can dynamically generate quests and storylines, ensuring each playthrough offers fresh and engaging challenges. This keeps players invested and provides a more personalized gaming experience. By analyzing player behavior and preferences, AI tailors quests to different playstyles, making the game more immersive and enjoyable.

When it comes to character behavior and interactions, AI is a game-changer. **Non-player characters (NPCs)** have traditionally followed scripted behaviors, which can make them predictable and less engaging. AI uses machine learning models to create adaptive and intelligent NPCs that learn from player actions and adjust their behavior. For example, in ***The Elder Scrolls V: Skyrim***, AI-driven NPCs exhibit dynamic behaviors that respond to the player's actions. If you steal something, NPCs may react suspiciously the next time they see you. This level of interactivity adds depth to the game, making the world feel alive and responsive.

AI isn't just about creating content; it also ensures the quality of the final product. Game testing and quality assurance are crucial but often labor-intensive. AI-driven bots can automate playtesting, identifying bugs and issues quickly. These bots can simulate thousands of playthroughs in a fraction of the time it would take human testers. Machine learning models can also predict potential game balance issues by analyzing gameplay data, ensuring a well-balanced and enjoyable experience. Google's DeepMind has been used to test complex game environments, helping developers identify and address potential issues before a game's release.

Player personalization is another area where AI excels, tailoring gaming experiences to individual preferences. By analyzing player behavior, AI can adjust difficulty levels dynamically, ensuring that the game remains challenging yet enjoyable for players of all skill levels. AI also powers personalized game recommendations, helping players discover new games that match their interests. In educational games, AI-driven adaptive learning systems analyze how players interact with the game, adjusting content to suit their learning pace and style. This makes learning more engaging and effective.

18

RESOURCES AND TOOLS FOR FURTHER EXPLORATION

Imagine you're about to bake a cake for the first time. You have all the ingredients laid out, but without a recipe, the process feels overwhelming. Now, think of AI as that cake and the tools and platforms we'll explore in this chapter as your recipe. These resources will guide you step-by-step, making the world of AI accessible, whether you're just starting or looking to deepen your knowledge. They cater to all levels of experience, ensuring you have the support you need to succeed.

TOP AI PLATFORMS AND TOOLS TO EXPLORE

When diving into AI, having the right tools is crucial. Fortunately, several comprehensive platforms accommodate various skill levels, from beginners to seasoned professionals.

- **Google's TensorFlow**: This versatile and robust open-source library is a cornerstone for machine learning and AI. TensorFlow offers a comprehensive ecosystem for building and training models, deploying machine learning applications, and managing data. It's especially useful for creating complex neural networks or exploring deep learning. With extensive documentation and strong community support, TensorFlow is ideal for both novices and experts.

- **Microsoft's Azure Machine Learning**: This cloud-based service provides a range of tools for building, training, and deploying machine learning models. Azure Machine Learning is particularly appealing for businesses and developers because it offers scalable infrastructure, detailed analytics, and integration with other Microsoft services. Its drag-and-drop interface simplifies model-building, making it accessible even for those with limited coding experience. It also supports various programming languages, including Python and R.
- **Google's Teachable Machine**: For those new to AI, Teachable Machine offers a gentle introduction. This user-friendly tool allows you to create machine-learning models without any coding. You can train models to recognize images, sounds, and poses using an interactive interface. For example, you might train a model to distinguish between different fruits by uploading images of apples, bananas, and oranges. The platform guides you through data collection, model training, and testing, making it an excellent starting point for learning about machine learning.
- **Lobe**: Another intuitive platform for beginners, Lobe specializes in building custom image classification models through a drag-and-drop interface. It simplifies machine learning by automating much of the process. You can import images, categorize them, and train your model with just a few clicks. Lobe also allows you to export your model to various platforms, including web and mobile

applications, making it easy for anyone to start with AI, regardless of their technical background.

As you become more comfortable with AI, you might want to explore specialized tools tailored for specific tasks:

- **Hugging Face Transformers**: This library focuses on natural language processing (NLP) and offers pretrained models for tasks like text classification, translation, and sentiment analysis. Hugging Face provides user-friendly APIs that make it easy to integrate these models into your projects. It's particularly beneficial for developers interested in creating applications that understand and generate human language, such as chatbots or content summarizers.
- **OpenCV**: For those interested in computer vision, OpenCV is a powerful library for image and video analysis. It includes modules for object detection, facial recognition, and image transformation. Widely used in robotics, security, and medical imaging, OpenCV offers extensive documentation and an active community. Whether you're developing a security system that recognizes faces or a medical application that analyzes X-rays, OpenCV has the tools you need.

Collaboration and sharing are key aspects of AI development, and several platforms facilitate these activities:

- **Google Colab**: This cloud-based **Jupyter Notebook** environment allows you to write and execute **Python** code in your browser. Colab comes preinstalled with popular machine learning libraries like TensorFlow, making it easy to get started. Its collaborative features enable multiple users to work on the same notebook simultaneously, making it ideal for team projects, educational purposes, or experimenting with AI without setting up a local environment.

- **Kaggle**: This community platform for data science and machine learning enthusiasts offers a space to share datasets, participate in competitions, and collaborate on projects. Kaggle's competitions tackle real-world challenges, providing a practical way to apply your AI skills. The platform also features an extensive repository of public datasets and code notebooks, which are excellent learning resources. Whether you want to test your skills in a competitive environment or collaborate on open-source projects, Kaggle provides a supportive and resource-rich community.

Interactive Element: AI Exploration Checklist

1. **Explore TensorFlow**. Visit the TensorFlow website, browse through the tutorials, and try building a simple neural network.
2. **Experiment with Azure Machine Learning**. Sign up for a free Azure account, explore the machine learning services, and create your first model using the drag-and-drop interface.
3. **Try Teachable Machine**. Go to the Teachable Machine website, upload some images, and train a model to recognize different objects.
4. **Use Lobe**. Download Lobe to import images and create a custom image classification model. Experiment with exporting the model to different platforms.

5. **Dive into Hugging Face Transformers**. Visit the Hugging Face website, explore the pretrained models, and try performing a text classification task.
6. **Explore OpenCV**. Install OpenCV, follow the introductory tutorials, and try implementing a simple object detection program.
7. **Collaborate on Google Colab**. Create a new notebook on Google Colab, invite a friend to collaborate, and work on a small project together.
8. **Join Kaggle**. Sign up for a Kaggle account, explore the datasets, and participate in a competition to apply your AI skills.

These resources and tools provide a solid foundation for exploring AI. Whether you're just starting or looking to expand your knowledge, these platforms offer the guidance and support needed for success. Embrace the opportunity to learn, experiment, and collaborate, and you'll find that AI is more accessible and exciting than you ever imagined.

ONLINE COMMUNITIES AND COURSES FOR AI ENTHUSIASTS

Joining online communities can greatly enhance your journey in AI. These platforms offer spaces to connect with like-minded individuals, share knowledge, and seek support.

- **Reddit's r/MachineLearning**: This subreddit is a vibrant hub where AI enthusiasts, researchers, and professionals discuss a wide range of topics. Whether you're curious about the latest research, need help with a project, or want to share insights, r/MachineLearning provides a welcoming environment with a diverse range of expertise.

- **AI Alignment Forum**: Focused on the safety and ethical implications of AI, this platform invites thoughtful discussions on developing AI systems that are both beneficial and safe. Attracting ethicists, researchers, and practitioners, the forum is ideal for those concerned about AI's ethical dimensions and who want to contribute to meaningful conversations.

For formalizing your learning, online courses offer structured education in AI:

- **Coursera's "Machine Learning" by Andrew Ng**: This highly recommended course provides a thorough introduction to machine learning concepts, including supervised and unsupervised learning, neural networks, and support vector machines. Andrew Ng's clear and engaging teaching style makes complex topics accessible, making this course a solid foundation for beginners.
- **edX's "AI for Everyone" by Andrew Ng**: For a nontechnical introduction to AI, this course covers the basics of AI, its applications, and its societal implications. It's designed for business leaders, policymakers, and anyone curious about AI's impact on various sectors, making it approachable and relevant to a broad audience.
- **Udacity's "Deep Learning Nanodegree"**: This advanced program focuses on neural networks and deep learning. It covers building neural networks and implementing **generative adversarial networks (GANs)** with hands-on projects that provide practical experience. Completing this nanodegree equips you with advanced skills highly sought after in the AI industry.
- **MIT's "Artificial Intelligence: Principles and Techniques"**: For those ready to dive deeper, this course

explores the theoretical foundations of AI, including search algorithms, machine learning, and probabilistic models. It's designed for individuals with a strong background in mathematics and programming and is ideal for those aiming for advanced roles or research in AI.

Attending AI events and conferences can further enhance your understanding and provide valuable networking opportunities:

- **NeurIPS (Conference on Neural Information Processing Systems)**: A leading AI conference that attracts top researchers and practitioners from around the world, presenting the latest advancements in AI research. It includes workshops, tutorials, and poster sessions, offering a comprehensive view of AI's current state.
- **AI Expo**: This industry-focused event showcases practical AI applications across sectors like healthcare, finance, and retail. Featuring keynote speeches, panel discussions, and exhibitions, the AI Expo offers insights into successful implementations and opportunities for networking with professionals driving AI innovation.

Engaging with these online communities, courses, and events can significantly enhance your AI journey. They provide opportunities to learn, connect, and grow, regardless of your current expertise. By immersing yourself in these resources, you can stay updated with the latest developments, gain new skills, and become part of a supportive and vibrant AI community.

GO BEYOND PRACTICALITY, COST-SAVINGS, AND TIME-EFFICIENCY AND START USING AI TO DO GOOD!

Congratulations on completing this comprehensive guide to harnessing AI in your everyday work and home life. I hope you are excited by the knowledge that this technology is about so much more than making more money, excelling at your profession, and delving into your creativity. In the second half of this book, you saw that AI can also be a catalyst for positive social change. It is already a tool in numerous impactful areas such as environmental sustainability, healthcare, and education. What's more, it boasts a huge potential in microfinancing, bias detection, and humanitarian work.

I hope I have inspired you to create art, break down language barriers, or think about how to harness AI to back the social causes you believe in. In fact, you can do your share for people in your community and beyond simply by sharing what you think of this book.

Thanks so much for your support. We are stronger together, and AI can knock down many barriers to help us connect more profoundly and meaningfully.

Scan the QR code below

CONCLUSION

As we wrap up our journey together, let's take a moment to reflect on the path we've traveled. We started by demystifying artificial intelligence, breaking down complex concepts into clear and understandable insights. From learning the basics of AI to exploring its surprising applications in healthcare, entertainment, and smart homes, we've covered a great deal of ground.

We examined how AI is revolutionizing healthcare, enhancing diagnostic accuracy, personalizing treatment plans, and speeding up drug discovery. In the world of entertainment, we discovered how AI personalizes content and creates immersive experiences, making our leisure time more enjoyable. In smart homes, AI brings convenience, security, and energy efficiency, transforming our daily routines into seamless experiences.

We also explored hands-on AI applications, including beginner-friendly tools and simple DIY projects that make AI accessible to everyone. But our journey didn't stop there. We tackled the ethical considerations of AI, addressing issues like bias, privacy, and the need for responsible AI development.

Throughout our exploration, we saw how AI is reshaping the job market. While it brings automation, it also creates new opportunities and roles, highlighting the importance of continuous learning. We delved into AI innovations and future trends in autonomous vehicles, climate change solutions, and space exploration.

Here are the key takeaways from our journey: AI is not a distant future; it's here and now, influencing various aspects of our lives. It has the power to enhance our abilities, streamline processes, and offer personalized experiences. However, it also comes with ethical responsibilities. Ensuring fairness, transparency, and accountability in AI systems is crucial. We must embrace AI while remaining mindful of its implications.

As we conclude, I encourage you to take the next steps in your AI journey. Whether you're a beginner or have more experience, there are numerous resources and tools available to expand your knowledge. Experiment with AI platforms like TensorFlow or beginner-friendly tools like Teachable Machine. Engage with online communities and take advantage of courses to deepen your understanding.

Remember, AI is a field of continuous learning and innovation. Stay curious, seek out new information, and don't hesitate to dive into AI projects. Your involvement can make a significant impact, whether in personal productivity, creative arts, or even tackling global challenges.

I want to express my heartfelt gratitude for joining me on this journey. Thank you for trusting me as your guide through the fascinating world of AI. Your willingness to learn and explore showcases the human spirit of curiosity and innovation.

Let's end on an optimistic note. The future of AI is bright and full of promise. It holds the potential to address some of humanity's most pressing issues, from healthcare to climate change. As AI continues to evolve, it will open new doors and create opportunities we can't yet imagine. You have the power to shape this future. By embracing AI responsibly and ethically, you can contribute to a world where technology enhances our lives and fosters a more inclusive society.

In conclusion, our journey through the world of AI has been enlightening and transformative. We've explored its applications, addressed its ethical considerations, and recognized its potential. As you move forward, carry these lessons with you. Stay engaged, stay curious, and be a part of the exciting future that AI promises. Together, we can harness the power of AI to make our lives better, smarter, and more connected. The possibilities are endless, and the future is yours to shape.

REFERENCES

"AI and Space Exploration | Department of Rocket Science," December 6, 2023. https://drupaldemo.harvardsites.harvard.edu/news/2023/12/ai-and-space-exploration.

"ETHICALLY ALIGNED DESIGN." IEEE, n.d. https://standards.ieee.org/wp-content/uploads/import/documents/other/ead_v2.pdf.

"GPT-3 Creative Fiction," June 19, 2020. https://gwern.net/gpt-3.

"The Impact of the General Data Protection Regulation (GDPR) on Artificial Intelligence." European Parliament, June 2020. https://www.europarl.europa.eu/RegData/etudes/STUD/2020/641530/EPRS_STU(2020)641530_EN.pdf.

"Top 10 AI-Powered Antivirus Programs of 2022," February 29, 2024. https://www.toolify.ai/ai-news/top-10-aipowered-antivirus-programs-of-2022-2206263.

Abbot, Henry. "Creating Art Using Generative Adversarial Networks." Kenyon College, n.d. https://digital.kenyon.edu/cgi/viewcontent.cgi?article=1012&context=dh_iphs_ai.

Akgun, Selin, and Christine Greenhow. "Artificial Intelligence in Education: Addressing Ethical Challenges in K-12 Settings." *Ai and Ethics* 2, no. 3 (2022): 431–40. https://doi.org/10.1007/s43681-021-00096-7.

Ali, Rashid. "Revolutionizing Primary Education in Rural India: The Role of AI." IndiaAI, January 8, 2024. https://indiaai.gov.in/article/revolutionizing-primary-education-in-rural-india-the-role-of-ai.

Anjaria, Pranav, Varun Asediya, Prakrutik Bhavsar, Abhishek Pathak, Dhruv Desai, and Veerupaxagouda Patil. "Artificial Intelligence in Public Health: Revolutionizing Epidemiological Surveillance for Pandemic Preparedness and Equitable Vaccine Access." *Vaccines* 11, no. 7 (June 26, 2023): 1154. https://doi.org/10.3390/vaccines11071154.

Artificial Intelligence. n.d. "AI Quotes in Business Impact." Accessed December 20, 2024. https://www.salesforce.com/artificial-intelligence/ai-quotes/https://www.dwassetmgmt.com/blog/an-investment-in-knowledge-pays-the-best-interest-benjamin-franklin

Baig, Anas. "The Impact of the GDPR on Artificial Intelligence." Securiti, March 10, 2024. https://securiti.ai/impact-of-the-gdpr-on-artificial-intelligence/.

Baldwin, Chris. "10 Best AI Personalization Tools for Websites, Apps, Email, and More." *Insider* (blog), November 10, 2023. https://useinsider.com/ai-personalization-tools/.

Bhide, Rucha. "Learn AI Together Community." Towards AI, July 29, 2024. https://towardsai.net/community.

Biswal, Avijeet. "Top 24 Artificial Intelligence Applications for 2025." Simplilearn.com, December 18, 2024. https://www.simplilearn.com/tutorials/artificial-intelligence-tutorial/artificial-intelligence-applications.

Branwen, Gwern. "GPT-3 Creative Fiction," June 19, 2020. https://gwern.net/gpt-3.

Capitol Technology Universiy. "The Ethical Considerations of Artificial Intelligence," n.d. https://www.captechu.edu/blog/ethical-considerations-of-artificial-intelligence.

Chan, Grace. "AI and Space Exploration | Department of Rocket Science." Harvard University, December 6, 2023. https://drupaldemo.harvardsites.harvard.edu/news/2023/12/ai-and-space-exploration.

Chetan, Rishav. "Navigating AI Transparency with Explainable AI Systems." Tredence, April 16, 2024. https://www.tredence.com/blog/$slug.

Claned. "The Role of AI in Personalized Learning." *Claned* (blog), April 12, 2024. https://claned.com/the-role-of-ai-in-personalized-learning/.

Conrad, Ryan. "AI Solutions for Real-Time Tracking & Visibility in Logistics." RTS Labs, March 1, 2024. https://rtslabs.com/ai-solutions-real-time-tracking-logistics/.

Cottray, Olivier. "Drone Mapping in Mozambique Helps Find Flood Victims, with AI Assistance." *Esri* (blog), November 10, 2022. https://www.esri.com/about/newsroom/blog/mozambique-drone-mapping-flood-victims/.

Crouse, Megan. "The 10 Best AI Courses That Are Worth Taking." TechRepublic, May 7, 2024. https://www.techrepublic.com/article/best-ai-courses/.

Dilmegani, Cem. "Top 25 Chatbot Case Studies & Success Stories." AIMultiple: High Tech Use Cases & Tools to Grow Your Business, December 21, 2024. https://research.aimultiple.com/top-chatbot-success/.

Ditto. "AI for Music Production: 10 Tools to Produce Like a Pro," January 9, 2024. https://dittomusic.com/en/blog/ai-for-music-production-tools-for-musicians.

elburz. "Interactive Art Examples." *The Interactive & Immersive HQ* (blog), March 6, 2024. https://interactiveimmersive.io/blog/interactive-media/interactive-art-examples/.

Gobi, S. "The Impact of AI on the Job Market: Trends, Statistics, and Future Prospects." LinkedIn, March 20, 2024. https://www.linkedin.com/pulse/impact-ai-job-market-trends-statistics-future-prospects-gobi-s-vch3c.

Habash, Fouad. "How Is Artificial Intelligence Changing the Translation Services

Industry?" Localization Services by BLEND, September 11, 2023. https://www.getblend.com/blog/artificial-intelligence-changing-the-translation-services-industry/.

Hao, Karen. "This Is How AI Bias Really Happens—and Why It's so Hard to Fix." MIT Technology Review, February 4, 2019. https://www.technologyreview.com/2019/02/04/137602/this-is-how-ai-bias-really-happensand-why-its-so-hard-to-fix/.

Harvard Business Review. "Collaborative Intelligence: Humans and AI Are Joining Forces." July 1, 2018. https://hbr.org/2018/07/collaborative-intelligence-humans-and-ai-are-joining-forces.

Henkin, David. "How To Future-Proof Your Career—Surviving In The AI Era." Forbes, May 10, 2024. https://www.forbes.com/sites/davidhenkin/2024/05/09/how-to-future-proof-your-career-surviving-in-the-ai-era/.

IBM. n.d. "Data Suggests Growth in Enterprise Adoption of AI is Due to Widespread Deployment by Early Adopters, But Barriers Keep 40% in the Exploration and Experimentation Phases." Accessed December 20, 2024. https://newsroom.ibm.com/2024-01-10-Data-Suggests-Growth-in-Enterprise-Adoption-of-AI-is-Due-to-Widespread-Deployment-by-Early-Adopters

IBM Blog. "Fantasy Football Trades: How IBM Granite Foundation Models Drive Personalized Explainability for Millions," October 15, 2024. https://www.ibm.com/blog/.

IBM. "AI Bias Examples," August 21, 2024. https://www.ibm.com/think/topics/shedding-light-on-ai-bias-with-real-world-examples.

Infosys Limited. "Fraud Detection Using AI in Banking." Infosys BPM, n.d. https://www.infosysbpm.com/blogs/bpm-analytics/fraud-detection-with-ai-in-banking-sector.html.

Invisibly. "Behind The Scenes of The Netflix Recommendation Algorithm." Invisibly, November 10, 2021. https://www.invisibly.com/learn-blog/netflix-recommendation-algorithm/.

Irvine, Robert. "How to Create a Machine Learning Model With Microsoft Lobe." MUO, November 12, 2020. https://www.makeuseof.com/create-machine-learning-model-microsoft-lobe/.

Jones, Jenny. "Case Study: Integrating AI into the Clinical Workflow." American College of Radiology, n.d. https://www.acr.org/-/media/ACR/Files/Case-Studies/V7_Integrating-AI.pdf.

Julia Angwin, Jeff Larson, Surya Mattu, and Lauren Kirchner, ProPublica. "Machine Bias." ProPublica, May 23, 2016. https://www.propublica.org/article/machine-bias-risk-assessments-in-criminal-sentencing.

Karim, Shoaib. "How AI Can Lead to Personalized Medicine | Insurance Thought

Leadership." Insurance Thought Leadership.com, June 6, 2024. https://www.insurancethoughtleadership.com/life-health/how-ai-can-lead-personalized-medicine.

Kuziemsky, Craig, Anthony J. Maeder, Oommen John, Shashi B. Gogia, Arindam Basu, Sushil Meher, and Marcia Ito. "Role of Artificial Intelligence within the Telehealth Domain." *Yearbook of Medical Informatics* 28, no. 1 (August 2019): 35–40. https://doi.org/10.1055/s-0039-1677897.

Capitol Technology University. "The Ethical Considerations of Artificial Intelligence," n.d. https://www.captechu.edu/blog/ethical-considerations-of-artificial-intelligence.

Law, Marcus. "Amazon Warehouse Robot Uses AI to Handle Millions of Items." Technology Magazine, November 15, 2022. https://technologymagazine.com/articles/amazon-warehouse-robot-uses-ai-to-handle-millions-of-items.

LinkedIn. "The Impact of AI on the Job Market: Trends, Statistics, and Future Prospects," n.d. https://www.linkedin.com/pulse/impact-ai-job-market-trends-statistics-future-prospects-gobi-s-vch3c.

Magyar, Robin. "Artificial Intelligence's Role in Supply Chain Risk Management." Everstream Analytics, February 15, 2023. https://www.everstream.ai/articles/artificial-intelligence-role-in-supply-chain-risk-management/.

Marr, Bernard. "12 New Jobs For The Generative AI Era." LinkedIn, February 5, 2024. https://www.linkedin.com/pulse/12-new-jobs-generative-ai-era-bernard-marr-z7bge.

Marr, Bernard. "15 Amazing Real-World Applications Of AI Everyone Should Know About." Forbes, n.d. https://www.forbes.com/sites/bernardmarr/2023/05/10/15-amazing-real-world-applications-of-ai-everyone-should-know-about/.

Marr, Bernard. "Starbucks: Using Big Data, Analytics And Artificial Intelligence To Boost Performance." Forbes, May 28, 2018. https://www.forbes.com/sites/bernardmarr/2018/05/28/starbucks-using-big-data-analytics-and-artificial-intelligence-to-boost-performance/.

Masterson, Victoria. " 9 Ways AI Is Helping Tackle Climate Change." World Economic Forum, February 12, 2024. https://www.weforum.org/agenda/2024/02/ai-combat-climate-change/.

Musani, Parvez. "Decking the Aisles with Data: How Walmart's AI-Powered Inventory System Brightens the Holidays." Walmart Global Tech, October 25, 2023. https://one.walmart.com/content/walmart-global-tech/en_us/blog/post/walmarts-ai-powered-inventory-system-brightens-the-holidays.html.

NICHES, NEW's &. "AI in Home Automation: Smart Homes of the Future." *Medium* (blog), September 16, 2023. https://medium.com/@mohsinali73a/ai-in-home-automation-smart-homes-of-the-future-5f49c9215dac.

O'Neill, Eimear. "Wealthsimple vs. Betterment (2023): In-Depth Comparison." Tokenist, January 8, 2024. https://tokenist.com/investing/wealthsimple-vs-betterment/.

Palo Alto Networks. "What Is the Role of AI in Threat Detection?" n.d. https://www.paloaltonetworks.com/cyberpedia/ai-in-threat-detection.

Paoli, P. "History of AI - First Chapter: From Turing to McCarthy." Pigro, September 7, 2021. https://blog.pigro.ai/en/history-of-artificial-intelligence.

Parsani, Puran. "Beauty and the Bot: How Sephora Reimagined Customer Experience with AI." Cut The Saas, February 23, 2024. https://www.cut-the-saas.com/ai/beauty-and-the-bot-how-sephora-reimagined-customer-experi ence-with-ai.

Parsons, Lian. "Ethical Concerns Mount as AI Takes Bigger Decision-Making Role." Harvard Gazette, October 26, 2020. https://news.harvard.edu/gazette/story/2020/10/ethical-concerns-mount-as-ai-takes-bigger-decision-making-role/.

Pavitra, M. "11 Best AI Translator Tools for Accurate Translations in 2025." ClickUp, December 1, 2024. https://clickup.com/blog/ai-translation-tools/.

Pazzanese, Christina. "Ethical Concerns Mount as AI Takes Bigger Decision-Making Role." Harvard Gazette, October 26, 2020. https://news.harvard.edu/gazette/story/2020/10/ethical-concerns-mount-as-ai-takes-bigger-decision-making-role/.

Pinto-Coelho, Luís. "How Artificial Intelligence Is Shaping Medical Imaging Technology: A Survey of Innovations and Applications." *Bioengineering* 10, no. 12 (December 18, 2023): 1435. https://doi.org/10.3390/bioengineer ing10121435.

ProjectPro. "30+ Artificial Intelligence Project Ideas for Beginners [2025]." ProjectPro, December 10, 2024. https://www.projectpro.io/article/artificial-intelligence-project-ideas/461.

R.P.F. "Narrow AI vs General AI and Super AI: How Do They Differ? - How to Learn Machine Learning," April 23, 2023. https://howtolearnmachinelearning.com/articles/narrow-ai-vs-general-ai/, https://howtolearnmachinelearning.com/articles/narrow-ai-vs-general-ai/.

Rambus Press. "The Algorithms of No Man's Sky." Rambus, May 17, 2016. https://www.rambus.com/blogs/the-algorithms-of-no-mans-sky-2/.

Ricci. "Evolving Education: The Impact Of AI And VR Technology On The Future Of Learning." eLearning Industry, March 27, 2023. https://elearningindustry.com/evolving-education-the-impact-of-ai-and-vr-technology-on-the-future-of-learning.

Ross, Casey. "Opening the 'Black Box,' Google DeepMind AI System Diagnoses Eye Diseases and Shows Its Work." *STAT* (blog), August 13, 2018. https://www.statnews.com/2018/08/13/google-deepmind-ai-diagnoses-eye-diseases/.

Rothmund, Felix, and Karthikeyan Jayaraman. "How AI Is Supercharging Money Management." Invite, n.d. https://www.intive.com/insights/how-ai-is-supercharging-money-management.

RuchaBhide. "Community | Towards AI," July 29, 2024. https://towardsai.net/community.

ScriptBook. "Democratizing Storytelling through the Art of AI," n.d. https://www.scriptbook.io.

Sean, Corp. "How Disney's The Lion King Became a Pioneer in the Use of Virtual Reality." *Center for Academic Innovation* (blog), March 6, 2020. https://ai.umich.edu/blog-posts/how-disneys-the-lion-king-became-a-pioneer-in-the-use-of-virtual-reality/.

Shah-Neville, Willow. "Five AI Drug Discovery Companies You Should Know About." *Labiotech.Eu* (blog), January 5, 2024. https://www.labiotech.eu/best-biotech/ai-drug-discovery-companies/.

Simplilearn.com. "Top 24 Artificial Intelligence Applications for 2025."https://www.simplilearn.com/tutorials/artificial-intelligence-tutorial/artificial-intelligence-applications.

Sivek, Susan Currie. "The 7 Best AI Platforms: Your Guide to Making a Smart Investment." Pecan AI, March 7, 2024. https://www.pecan.ai/blog/best-ai-platforms-guide/.

Stefanovic, Maja. "2023 in Review: This Year's Breakthroughs in Automated Driving | HERE," November 7, 2023. https://www.here.com/learn/blog/automated-driving-trends-2023.

StoryLab.ai. "Scale Up Your Social Media Personalization With These 5 AI Techniques." StoryLab.ai, July 7, 2024. https://storylab.ai/ai-for-personalizing-social-media-content-at-scale/.

Teachable Machine. "Teachable Machine," n.d. https://teachablemachine.withgoogle.com/.

Team DigitalDefynd. "AI in the Pharmaceutical Industry [5 Success Stories][2024]." *DigitalDefynd* (blog), February 26, 2024. https://digitaldefynd.com/IQ/ai-in-pharmaceutical-industry/.

Team Sanction Scanner. "Artificial Intelligence and Anti-Money Laundering - Sanction Scanner." Sanction Scanner, November 13, 2019. https://www.sanctionscanner.com/blog/artificial-intelligence-and-anti-money-laundering-17.

Toolify.ai. "How to Create an AI Chatbot with ChatFuel," January 9, 2024. https://www.toolify.ai/ai-news/how-to-create-an-ai-chatbot-with-chatfuel-468187.

Trust Community. "ISO 42001 Framework," May 7, 2024. https://community.trustcloud.ai/docs/grc-launchpad/grc-101/compliance/iso-42001-framework-ensuring-safety-consistency-and-accountability-with-ai/.

Wanders, Achim. "AI in Education: Squirrel AI vs. Carnegie Learning 📚 -

Personalized Learning Approaches." MathAware Nude AI Generators & NSFW, January 9, 2024. https://www.mathaware.org/ai-in-education-squirrel-ai-vs-carnegie-learning-personalized-learning-approaches/.

Wordly. "Real-Time Translation | Powered by Wordly.Ai," n.d. https://www.wordly.ai/real-time-translation

ABOUT THE AUTHOR

Albert Hsu is most known as a successful investment manager with extensive experience working with foundations, pension funds, and funds of funds. As a private investor, he has demonstrated exceptional skill in identifying promising opportunities in the cryptocurrency space. A graduate of the prestigious Bronx High School of Science, Albert has a diverse educational background, holding degrees in economics, computer science, and classical archaeology. This unique blend of quantitative and qualitative expertise provides him with a profound understanding of how technology can drive transformative change in the world.

www.ingramcontent.com/pod-product-compliance
Lightning Source LLC
LaVergne TN
LVHW022053200926
848481LV00003B/891
9798218670412